SCOTT M. FRALEY

Stock Market for Beginners

A Step-by-Step Guide to Understanding Stock Market Investing, Maximizing Returns Through Trading Strategies, Building a Strong Investment Portfolio for Long-Term Gain

This book was professionally typeset on Reedsy.
Find out more at reedsy.com

Contents

Introduction

Imagine being able to build a secure financial future for yourself by making informed investment decisions in the stock market. It might sound like something only seasoned investors or financial experts can achieve, but that's far from the truth. This book is crafted specifically with you in mind: whether you're a working professional juggling career responsibilities and personal life commitments or a college student or recent graduate brimming with ambition and dreams of future success. My goal is to empower you to take control of your finances and set the stage for your long-term financial growth and security.

Investing in the stock market isn't just about putting your money into various stocks and hoping for the best. It's an incredible journey towards financial independence and growth. Have you ever thought about what it would be like to not worry about unexpected expenses or having enough saved up for major life milestones? By understanding the fundamental concepts and strategies of the stock market, you'll be well-equipped to make wise investment decisions that could potentially grow your wealth over time. This knowledge doesn't just fill your bank account; it's a valuable asset in achieving your financial aspirations and dreams.

The importance of learning about the stock market cannot be overstated, especially in today's fast-paced, ever-evolving economic landscape. Whether aiming to save up for your dream home, planning for a comfortable retirement, or simply wanting to create a buffer against financial uncertainties, investing wisely can help you reach those goals. The stock market, particularly when approached with knowledge and strategy, offers opportunities for returns that savings accounts and other traditional methods fall short of providing. Unlike a paycheck that stops as soon as you leave your job, smart investments can continue to generate income even as you sleep.

So, where do we begin this exciting journey? Picture this book as your personal guide, taking you step-by-step through the essential aspects of stock market investing. We start with foundational terms because, let's face it, the financial world has its own language that can be intimidating at first. But don't worry—once you understand the basics, things will start to make a lot more sense. We'll break down complex jargon into simple, relatable concepts. You'll learn what stocks are, how the stock market operates, and why the prices of stocks fluctuate.

From there, we'll delve into various investment strategies. You'll discover how to analyze stock performance, understand market trends, and recognize the signs of a good investment. Importantly, we will also discuss the risks involved in stock market investments—because no investment is without risk—and how you can manage and mitigate these risks through thoughtful and informed decision-making.

Each chapter is designed to build upon the previous one, creating a comprehensive roadmap from novice to a confident investor. As you move through the book, you'll gain a deeper understanding of how to construct a diversified portfolio, balance risk versus reward, and leverage different types of accounts suited to your investing goals, whether they are short-term gains or long-term wealth accumulation.

Moreover, this journey isn't meant to be a passive reading experience. To truly benefit from the insights and strategies discussed, I encourage you to engage actively with the material. Real learning happens when you apply theoretical knowledge to real-life scenarios. Grab a notebook, jot down key pointers, reflect on them, and think about how they can be applied to your unique financial situation. Experiment with virtual trading platforms to get a feel for the market without risking actual money. This hands-on approach will significantly enhance your understanding and confidence in making informed investment decisions.

This book is not just a collection of facts and figures; it's a practical guide to transforming your financial outlook. Whether you're starting late or early, the strategies and information presented here are actionable, realistic, and aimed at helping you meet your financial objectives. We'll explore real-world examples and case studies to illustrate key points. These stories of successful (and occasionally unsuccessful) investors will offer insights into common pitfalls and highlight best practices.

Remember, investing in the stock market is not a get-rich-quick scheme. It requires patience, diligence, and sometimes a bit of faith in the process. There will be ups and downs, but with the right knowledge and mindset, you can navigate these fluctuations more effectively.

This journey you're about to embark on is one of empowerment. Taking charge of your financial future is a liberating experience. No longer will you feel anxious or uncertain about your financial status. Instead, you'll gain a sense of control and purpose as you make educated decisions aimed at growing your wealth and securing your financial future.

As you read through this book, keep an open mind and stay curious. Ask questions, seek out additional resources, and never stop learning. The world of stock market investing is vast and dynamic, but with the tools and knowledge provided in this book, you'll be well on your way to becoming a savvy investor. So let's get started on this exciting path towards financial independence and growth! Welcome to the world of stock market investing, where your financial dreams are within reach, and the journey to achieving them begins today.

Chapter 1: Introduction to the Stock Market

Understanding the stock market might seem like a daunting task for beginners, but it fundamentally revolves around the buying and selling of ownership shares in various businesses. These transactions take place in various markets where stock prices fluctuate continuously based on supply and demand dynamics. While it can appear complex, grasping the basics of how the stock market functions can open up opportunities for individuals to invest their money wisely and grow their wealth over time.

In this chapter, we will delve into the fundamental aspects of the stock market to provide you with a solid foundation. We will explore key concepts such as the difference between primary and secondary markets, shedding light on how companies raise funds through initial public offerings (IPOs) and how existing shares are traded among investors. We will also discuss the vital role that stock exchanges play in facilitating these trades and ensuring a regulated and transparent trading environment. Additionally, you will learn about the importance of market capitalization, which helps categorize companies into different groups and shapes investment strategies. By the end of this chapter, you will have a comprehensive understanding of the basic structure and functioning of the stock market, empowering you to make informed investment decisions.

1.1 What is the stock market?

The stock market plays a critical role in the financial world by facilitating the buying and selling of securities. At its core, the stock market is a collection of markets where stocks (pieces of ownership in businesses) are bought and sold. Each transaction in the stock market reflects the dynamic nature of supply and demand, influencing stock prices based on various factors like company performance and economic indicators. By providing a platform for these trades, the stock market helps companies raise capital by issuing shares to investors and offers individuals opportunities to invest and potentially grow their wealth.

A fundamental aspect of the stock market is the distinction between primary and secondary markets. The primary market refers to the issuance of new shares directly by a company during events like initial public offerings (IPOs). This process is crucial for companies looking to raise funds for expansion or other business needs. In contrast, the secondary market involves the trading of existing shares among investors. Once the shares are issued in the primary market, they can be freely bought and sold in the secondary market. This distinction is vital because it highlights how stocks move from being a method for companies to raise capital to a means for investors to trade and invest based on their market perceptions.

Stock exchanges play an essential role in facilitating trading activities within the stock market. These exchanges, such as the New York Stock Exchange (NYSE) and NASDAQ, provide a regulated environment where buyers and sellers can execute trades with confidence and efficiency. The exchanges ensure transparency by requiring listed companies to meet specific disclosure standards, thereby maintaining investor trust. Additionally, stock exchanges utilize advanced technology to match buy and sell orders quickly, which enhances liquidity and allows investors to convert their investments into cash readily. The presence of multiple stock exchanges also fosters competition, which can lead to better services and lower transaction costs for investors.

Market capitalization is another crucial concept within the stock market, representing the total market value of a company's outstanding shares. It's calculated by multiplying the current share price by the number of outstanding shares. Market capitalization is often used to categorize companies into different groups, such as large-cap, mid-cap, and small-cap. Understanding market capitalization helps investors assess a company's size and relative importance within the market. For instance, larger companies tend to have greater stability and are often included in major stock indices, while smaller companies may offer higher growth potential but come with increased risk.

The significance of market capitalization extends beyond categorization; it also impacts investment strategies and portfolio management. Investors often diversify their portfolios by including stocks from various market cap categories to balance risk and reward. Large-cap stocks typically provide steady returns and dividends, making them attractive for conservative investors. On the other hand, small-cap stocks can deliver substantial growth, appealing to those with higher risk tolerance. By considering market capitalization, investors can tailor their investment approach to align with their financial goals and risk appetite.

1.2 Functions of the stock market

The stock market serves as a crucial platform for companies to raise funds for business expansions. By issuing shares to the public, businesses can gather essential capital without incurring debt. This funding allows companies to invest in new projects, research and development, or enhance infrastructure. For instance, tech giants like Apple have historically used the stock market to fund innovative product lines, ensuring they stay ahead of competitors.

Moreover, when a company decides to go public through an Initial Public Offering (IPO), it opens up opportunities to accumulate large sums of money rapidly. These additional funds are often pivotal in scaling operations, entering new markets, or acquiring other businesses. The influx of capital from the public can significantly boost a company's growth trajectory, making the stock market an indispensable tool for corporate expansion. However, it's important for businesses to maintain transparency and good governance to attract and retain investor confidence.

In essence, the stock market not only provides a venue for corporations to secure necessary funds but also gives them a chance to enhance their public image. Being listed on prominent exchanges such as the NYSE or NASDAQ adds a layer of credibility, which can be advantageous in various business dealings. Thus, the stock market plays a multifaceted role in supporting and sustaining corporate growth and innovation.

For individual investors, participating in the stock market offers a unique opportunity to own a portion of a company. This ownership is represented by purchasing shares, which entitles investors to a fraction of the company's assets and earnings. Owning stocks allows individuals to potentially benefit from a company's success through capital appreciation and dividends. For example, early investors in companies like Tesla have seen substantial returns as the company grew exponentially.

Investing in stocks can also serve as a gateway to learning about different industries and understanding market dynamics. Engaging with the stock market encourages investors to stay informed about economic trends, industry developments, and corporate performance. This knowledge can not only aid in making more informed investment decisions but also contribute to overall financial literacy.

Furthermore, stock ownership empowers individuals to participate in shareholder meetings and vote on important company matters. This involvement provides a sense of participation in the company's governance and decision-making processes. Thus, the stock market democratizes investment, allowing individuals to directly influence and benefit from corporate success.

Economically, the stock market plays a crucial role in promoting

9

liquidity and efficient allocation of resources. Liquidity refers to how quickly an asset can be converted into cash without affecting its price. The stock market facilitates this by providing a platform where buyers and sellers can transact seamlessly, ensuring that equities can be easily traded at any given time.

Efficient allocation of resources is another key function of the stock market. It channels funds from savers who have excess capital to businesses that require it for productive use. By continuously assessing corporate performance and prospects, the stock market helps direct investments toward companies that promise better returns. This process ensures that resources are utilized optimally, fostering economic growth and innovation.

Additionally, the stock market's ability to reflect real-time information and collective sentiment about a company's future performance aids in price discovery. Investors base their buying and selling decisions on this information, thus ensuring that stock prices consistently represent the intrinsic value of underlying assets. This mechanism underpins a healthy and dynamic economy, as funds are continually reallocated to their most productive uses.

Investor education and risk management are paramount for anyone venturing into the stock market. Understanding the basics of investing and the inherent risks involved can significantly enhance one's chances of success. Educational resources, including books, online tutorials, and financial news outlets, provide valuable insights into market operations, investment strategies, and economic indicators.

Risk management involves diversifying one's investment portfolio to mitigate potential losses. Spreading investments across different asset classes, industries, and geographies can reduce exposure to a single security or sector's poor performance. Tools like stop-loss orders and hedging strategies further help in managing investment risks. These practices ensure that investors are prepared for market volatility and can protect their investments during downturns.

Moreover, recognizing the psychological aspects of investing is crucial. Emotional decision-making, driven by fear or greed, can lead to suboptimal investment choices. Developing a disciplined approach, sticking to a well-thought-out investment plan, and continuously educating oneself can foster long-term financial stability and growth. Hence, investor education and prudent risk management form the bedrock of successful stock market participation.

1.3 History of the stock market

The origins of stock trading can be traced back to ancient times when merchants and traders began pooling resources to share risks and profits. In the 1600s, the concept of joint-stock companies emerged in Europe, allowing investors to buy shares representing portions of a company's capital. The Dutch East India Company is often cited as one of the first examples, issuing shares that could be bought and sold among investors. This early form of stock trading provided a way to fund large ventures, such as expeditions or colony establishments, paving the way for modern-day stock markets.

As the idea of stock trading evolved, so did the need for more organized and formalized exchanges. The Amsterdam Stock Exchange, established in 1611, is considered the world's first official stock exchange. It created a more structured environment for trading shares and debts, offering investors greater security and regulated practices. Following this, other countries began setting up their own exchanges, such as the London Stock Exchange and the New York Stock Exchange, which formalized stock trading further with rules and regulations designed to protect investors and ensure fair trading practices.

Throughout its development, the stock market has seen significant milestones that have shaped its current form. The formation of large corporations in the late 19th and early 20th centuries led to an increased demand for capital and, subsequently, more widespread stock ownership. Innovations like ticker tapes and telegraph technology improved communication and information dissemination, making trading faster and more accessible. In recent decades, the advent of electronic trading platforms revolutionized the market once again, enabling global participation and real-time transactions, vastly increasing market liquidity and efficiency.

Key historical events have played crucial roles in shaping the trajectory of stock market evolution. The Great Depression of the 1930s had a profound impact on how stock markets operate, leading to stricter regulatory frameworks and oversight aimed at preventing market manipulation and protecting investors. Similarly, the economic reforms and technological advancements of the late 20th century spurred dramatic growth in global stock markets, integrating financial systems worldwide and fostering unprecedented levels of investment and corporate expansion.

Examining the role of these key historical events highlights the interconnectedness between stock markets and wider economic trends. For instance, the post-World War II economic boom saw an explosion in middle-class wealth, which translated into increased participation in stock markets by individual investors. Conversely, market crashes and economic downturns have underscored the volatility inherent in stock trading, emphasizing the need for robust risk management and investor education.

1.4 Global impact of stock markets

The stock markets have long been a powerful force in shaping economic growth and societal progress. Highlighting historical examples of market crashes provides insight into how deeply integrated these financial arenas are with broader economic health. For instance, the 1929 Wall Street Crash, which led to the Great Depression, underscores how significant downturns can wreak havoc on economies. Thousands of businesses failed, millions lost their jobs, and investor sentiment soured for years. Similarly, the 2008 financial crisis, triggered by the collapse of Lehman Brothers and subsequent market crash, had global repercussions, shaking confidence in financial institutions and causing widespread economic turmoil.

These crashes not only affect economies but also influence the behavior and sentiment of investors. When markets plummet, fear and uncertainty dominate, leading to panic selling and a reluctance to invest further. This cascading effect can exacerbate economic downturns as investors pull money out of markets, further decreasing liquidity and investment. Historically, recovery from such events often requires substantial government intervention and time to restore confidence and stability.

Despite the grim impact of market crashes, they also serve as valuable lessons for risk management and regulatory improvements. Post-crisis reforms, such as the establishment of the Securities and Exchange Commission (SEC) after the 1929 crash or the Dodd-Frank Act following the 2008 crisis, aim to mitigate future risks and protect both the economy and investors. These measures help build a more resilient financial system capable of supporting ongoing economic growth.

The interplay between stock market performance and broader economic indicators is another critical aspect to understand. The stock market often reflects the health of an economy, serving as a barometer for economic conditions. During times of economic prosperity, stock prices generally rise due to increased corporate profits and optimistic future expectations. Conversely, during economic downturns, stock prices tend to fall as companies' earnings prospects dim and investor confidence wanes.

It's essential to note that while stock markets provide crucial signals about economic trends, they don't always align perfectly with economic realities. Sometimes, markets may be buoyant despite underlying economic weaknesses, driven by factors like speculative trading or monetary policy interventions, such as low-interest rates boosting asset prices. Therefore, interpreting stock market movements requires a nuanced understanding of various influencing factors beyond just company performance, including geopolitical events, technological advancements, and shifts in consumer behavior.

Broader economic indicators, such as GDP growth rates, unemployment levels, and inflation rates, play significant roles in shaping market trends. Strong economic data usually bolsters investor confidence, leading to market rallies. On the other hand, negative economic news can trigger sell-offs, as seen in instances where disappointing job reports or unexpected inflation spikes lead to market volatility. Understanding this dynamic allows investors to make more informed decisions based on both market and economic analyses.

As we delve into the globalization of stock markets, it becomes evident how interconnected the world's financial systems have become. The advent of technology and electronic trading has enabled capital to flow freely across borders, creating a global marketplace where stocks from any country can be traded internationally. This interconnectedness has significant implications for economic growth, as it allows for greater access to capital and investment opportunities worldwide.

Globalization means that economic events in one part of the world can have immediate ripple effects across global markets. For example, a political crisis in Europe could spark sell-offs in Asian markets, which in turn affects the U.S. exchanges. This interdependence necessitates a global perspective when analyzing market trends and making investment decisions. Investors must consider not only domestic economic indicators but also international developments and their potential impacts on global financial systems.

The benefits of a globalized stock market include enhanced liquidity, diversification opportunities, and the ability to participate in the growth of emerging markets. However, it also introduces complexities and risks, such as currency fluctuations, geopolitical uncertainties, and varying regulatory environments. Navigating these challenges requires a thorough understanding of both local and global economic landscapes, as well as strategic risk management practices.

Major stock markets like the New York Stock Exchange (NYSE) and NASDAQ exert considerable influence on the global economy. As two of the largest and most active exchanges in the world, they set the tone for market behavior and investor sentiment globally. The NYSE, known for its stringent listing requirements and large corporations, represents the epitome of blue-chip stability. In contrast, the NASDAQ, home to many tech giants, symbolizes innovation and growth potential.

The performance of these major stock markets often serves as a benchmark for others around the world. Positive trends in the NYSE or NASDAQ can spur optimism and drive up indices in other countries. Conversely, downturns or crises within these exchanges can lead to global sell-offs, reflecting their central role in the financial ecosystem. Understanding how these markets operate and their relationship with smaller exchanges is key to grasping the broader picture of global financial health.

1.5 Wrapping It Up

We've delved deeply into the foundations of the stock market, exploring its structure, functions, historical development, and global impact. By now, you should have a clearer understanding of how this complex system operates and why it plays such a pivotal role in both corporate growth and individual wealth building.

Remember when we started, emphasizing that the stock market serves as a critical platform for buying and selling securities? We've seen how the primary and secondary markets function, providing pathways for companies to raise capital and for investors to trade their shares efficiently. Stock exchanges like the NYSE and NASDAQ offer regulated environments ensuring transparency and trust, enabling smooth transactions and liquidity.

Looking at market capitalization, you've learned how to categorize companies based on their size and understand the risks and rewards associated with investing in large-cap versus small-cap stocks. This insight is vital for making informed decisions that align with your financial goals and risk tolerance.

For those venturing into the stock market, it's essential to recognize both the opportunities and the inherent risks. While investing in stocks can yield high returns and offer a stake in the success of prominent companies, it also requires a solid grasp of market dynamics, economic indicators, and effective risk management strategies. Diversifying your portfolio and staying informed can help mitigate potential losses and enhance your investment experience.

The historical perspectives shared demonstrate not only the evolution of stock trading but also the lessons learned from past market crashes. Events like the 1929 Wall Street Crash and the 2008 financial crisis underscore the need for robust regulatory frameworks to protect investors and maintain market stability. These episodes also highlight the importance of investor education and prudent risk management practices.

On a broader scale, the stock market's performance often mirrors economic health, with rising stock prices reflecting prosperity and falling prices indicating downturns. However, keep in mind that market movements aren't always perfectly aligned with economic realities. Factors such as geopolitical events, technological advancements, and shifts in consumer behavior can also influence market trends.

Globalization has interconnected stock markets worldwide, allowing for seamless capital flow across borders. This interdependence means that economic events in one region can have immediate ripple effects globally. As an investor, considering international developments alongside domestic factors is crucial for a comprehensive analysis.

Navigating the complexities of a globalized stock market involves understanding the benefits and risks. Enhanced liquidity, diversification opportunities, and participation in emerging market growth are some advantages. However, challenges like currency fluctuations, geopolitical uncertainties, and varied regulatory environments require strategic planning and risk management.

As you move forward, think about the broader implications of your investments. Successful participation in the stock market can contribute not just to personal financial growth but also to economic innovation and societal progress. The knowledge gained here forms a strong foundation, equipping you to make informed decisions and navigate the intricacies of the stock market with confidence.

Keep in mind that the journey doesn't end here. Continuous learning, staying updated on market trends, and adapting to changing circumstances are key to long-term success. So, take what you've learned, apply it wisely, and look forward to the possibilities that the stock market holds for your future.

Chapter 2: Essential Terminology

Understanding essential stock market terminology is a fundamental step for anyone interested in navigating the financial markets. The stock market is filled with specialized terms and concepts that might seem confusing at first glance, but getting familiar with them can greatly enhance your investment journey. By learning these critical terms, you will be better prepared to make informed decisions and maximize the potential of your investments.

In this chapter, we will delve into various key terms related to stocks and shares, offering clear explanations to demystify these concepts. We will explore what stocks and shares represent, distinguishing between common and preferred stocks, and highlighting their unique characteristics. We'll also discuss different types of shares such as authorized, issued, and outstanding shares, and how these distinctions impact your investment strategy. By the end of this chapter, you'll have a solid grasp of the essential terminology needed to confidently participate in the stock market.

2.1 Stocks and Shares

Understanding the difference between stocks and shares is crucial for anyone looking to enter the stock market. Stocks represent ownership in a company and come with various benefits and responsibilities for the shareholders. When you purchase a stock, you own a part of that company, entitling you to a portion of its earnings and assets. This means that as the company grows and profits, so does the value of your investment, allowing you potential capital gains.

In addition to potential financial benefits through capital gains, owning stocks also grants shareholders voting rights on major company decisions. These decisions can range from electing board members to approving significant corporate changes. This involvement in the company's governance gives shareholders a sense of control over their investments and contributes to the overall corporate strategy and direction. By participating in these voting processes, shareholders can help shape the future of the companies they invest in.

Moreover, it's essential to understand the significance of differentiating between common and preferred stocks when making investment decisions. Common stocks are the most prevalent type of stock that investors buy. They provide ownership in a company and typically come with voting rights. However, dividends paid on common stocks are not guaranteed and can vary based on the company's performance. Preferred stocks, on the other hand, usually do not carry voting rights but offer fixed dividends. In times of liquidation, preferred shareholders have a higher claim on the company's assets than common shareholders, offering a slightly lower risk.

Knowing the distinction between common and preferred stocks helps investors make informed decisions about where to allocate their funds. For instance, those seeking stable income might prefer the consistent dividends of preferred stocks, while those willing to take on more risk for potentially higher returns might opt for common stocks. Understanding these differences can significantly influence an investor's portfolio balance and risk management strategies.

Shares, unlike stocks, denote specific units of ownership within a given company. Each share represents a fraction of the company's total equity. For example, if you own 100 shares of a company, it indicates the exact amount of your ownership stake. Owning shares comes with certain rights and responsibilities, such as the right to receive dividends (if declared by the company) and the obligation to adhere to any shareholder agreements.

The concept of shares provides a clearer picture of one's investment size in a company. Whether you hold one share or thousands, each share entitles you to a proportional part of the company's earnings and assets. This precise breakdown of ownership allows investors to gauge their level of investment accurately and strategically decide how much more they wish to invest or divest based on their financial goals.

Furthermore, understanding the different types of shares—authorized, issued, and outstanding—is critical in evaluating a company's ownership structure. Authorized shares are the maximum number of shares a company can legally issue, as approved by its corporate charter. Issued shares are those that the company has actually sold to investors, including both public and private investors. Outstanding shares refer to the shares currently held by all shareholders, including shares held by institutional investors and insiders.

Differentiating between these types of shares aids investors in assessing a company's financial health and decision-making processes. For instance, a company with a large number of authorized but unissued shares might be planning future financing rounds through additional stock offerings. Conversely, high levels of issued shares could indicate past capital-raising efforts. Evaluating these factors helps investors understand the company's growth strategy and potential dilution of shares, impacting their overall investment value.

To sum up, grasping the terminology around stocks and shares and recognizing the nuances between them is vital for anyone looking to navigate the stock market effectively. Stocks represent a broader ownership interest in a company with associated rights and potential financial benefits. Understanding the distinctions between common and preferred stocks can guide more tailored and strategic investment decisions. Meanwhile, shares concretely quantify ownership stakes within a company and come with specific rights and responsibilities that are crucial for managing one's investments.

2.2 Bonds and Mutual Funds

Bonds form a fundamental part of many investment portfolios, serving as debt securities issued by governments or corporations. When an investor buys a bond, they are essentially lending money to the issuer in exchange for periodic interest payments, known as coupon payments, and the return of the bond's face value at maturity. This relatively predictable stream of income makes bonds appealing for those seeking a steady, fixed income. For working professionals or recent graduates looking to start their investing journey, understanding bonds is crucial. They provide a balance to more volatile investments like stocks, thereby adding stability to an investment portfolio.

A key aspect of bonds is distinguishing between government and corporate bonds. Government bonds, often referred to as Treasuries in the United States, are issued by national governments and are considered low-risk because they are backed by the government's ability to tax its citizens and generate income. Corporate bonds, on the other hand, are issued by companies and carry a higher risk than government bonds because they depend on the company's financial health and ability to pay back the debt. Assessing these risks and understanding the potential returns can help investors make informed decisions about which types of bonds to include in their portfolios. Higher yields typically compensate for higher credit risk in corporate bonds, but the safety of government bonds might appeal more to conservative investors.

Evaluating bonds also involves understanding bond yields and their relationship with interest rates. Bond yields represent the annual return an investor can expect from holding a bond and are inversely related to interest rates. When interest rates rise, the prices of existing bonds typically fall, making their yields more attractive compared to new issues. Conversely, when interest rates fall, existing bonds with higher coupon rates become more valuable, increasing their prices and lowering their yields. For novice investors, grasping this relationship is vital for navigating the bond market effectively, especially during periods of fluctuating interest rates. It's worth noting that long-term bonds tend to be more sensitive to changes in interest rates compared to short-term bonds.

Mutual funds are another essential component of investment portfolios, providing a way for investors to pool their resources together. These pooled funds are then invested in diversified portfolios managed by professional fund managers. Mutual funds allow individual investors to access a wide variety of assets, including stocks, bonds, and other securities, which might be difficult to obtain individually due to high costs or complexity. This diversification helps reduce risk as the performance of different assets can offset each other, leading to more stable returns. For working professionals and recent graduates, mutual funds offer an accessible entry point into the world of investing, combining simplicity with diversification.

Understanding mutual fund fees and expenses is crucial for evaluating their cost-effectiveness. Mutual funds come with various fees, including management fees, administrative fees, and sometimes sales charges known as loads. These fees are expressed as an expense ratio, which indicates the percentage of the fund's assets used to cover these costs annually. High fees can significantly erode investment returns over time, making it imperative for investors to compare expense ratios across different mutual funds. Index funds, a type of mutual fund that passively tracks a market index, generally have lower fees compared to actively managed funds because they require fewer resources to manage.

Moreover, knowing how to interpret mutual fund performance metrics like net asset value (NAV) and expense ratio aids in assessing fund performance. NAV represents the per-share value of the fund's holdings and is calculated by dividing the total value of all securities in the portfolio by the number of outstanding shares. This metric helps investors understand the current value of their investment in the fund. Meanwhile, the expense ratio gives insight into the cost structure of the fund, helping investors gauge whether the fees charged justify the fund's performance. By carefully analyzing these metrics, investors can make more informed choices about which mutual funds align with their financial goals and risk tolerance.

2.3 Market Indices

When it comes to investing, understanding market indices is crucial for making informed decisions. Market indices serve as benchmarks representing a particular segment of the market, helping investors gauge its overall performance. Essentially, they provide a snapshot of how various sectors are faring at any given time.

A market index comprises a selected grouping of stocks, bonds, or other securities, reflecting the performance of that group.

This makes indices invaluable tools for both individual and institutional investors. They can track specific segments, such as technology stocks, or broader markets like all companies listed on a major exchange. By monitoring these indices, investors can quickly assess market trends and make timely investment choices.

Popular indices like the S&P 500 and Dow Jones Industrial Average (DJIA) are commonly referenced to gauge the health of the U.S. stock market. The S&P 500 includes 500 of the largest U.S. companies, providing a broad overview of the market's direction. With diversified industries, it offers insights into economic conditions and investor sentiment. On the other hand, the DJIA tracks 30 large, publicly-owned companies in various sectors, serving as an indicator of the industrial economy's health.

These indices have become essential benchmarks due to their lengthy histories and reliable representations of market movements. Investors often look to them when evaluating portfolio performance or making predictions about future market dynamics. Understanding their composition and methodology helps in comprehending broader economic indicators.

Exploring sector-specific indices allows investors to gain deeper insights into particular industries' performance. These indices focus on specific sectors such as technology, healthcare, or energy, enabling investors to track industry-specific trends. For example, the NASDAQ-100 focuses heavily on technology stocks, making it a go-to index for those interested in the tech sector.

Such specialized indices can provide more granular data, aiding investors in spotting opportunities and risks within particular fields. By examining these indices, investors can better understand which sectors are driving market growth and which might be facing challenges. This information is invaluable for constructing a well-diversified investment portfolio tailored to specific sector performance.

Index investing, a passive strategy involving tracking indices through index funds or exchange-traded funds (ETFs), has gained popularity due to its simplicity and effectiveness. Unlike active investing, where fund managers continuously buy and sell assets to outperform the market, index investors aim to replicate the returns of a specific index. This method leverages the stability and performance of established indices without the need for frequent trading.

One of the key benefits of index investing is diversification. By investing in an index fund, investors automatically gain exposure to a wide range of stocks within that index. This spreads out risk and reduces the impact of any single stock's poor performance on the overall portfolio. Additionally, because index funds require less hands-on management, they typically come with lower fees and expenses compared to actively managed funds.

Another advantage of index investing is its consistency. Index funds aim to match the performance of their underlying indices, offering steady returns that reflect broader market trends. This predictable approach can be particularly appealing for beginners looking to build a solid investment foundation without the complexities and uncertainties of active trading. Learning about these benefits can help investors make more informed choices and develop a balanced, cost-effective portfolio.

Understanding the concept of benchmarking is also critical for measuring investment performance. A benchmark serves as a standard against which the performance of a portfolio or fund can be compared. Market indices often function as these benchmarks since they represent a particular segment of the market or economy accurately.

By comparing their portfolio's returns to those of an appropriate index, investors can determine whether their investments are performing well or if adjustments are needed. For instance, if a portfolio consistently underperforms relative to its benchmark, it might signal the need for reallocation or strategy changes. Conversely, matching or exceeding the benchmark indicates that the current investment strategy is effective.

Investors must understand how to interpret index changes and correlate them with market trends to make informed decisions. For instance, significant movements in the S&P 500 or DJIA can reflect broader economic shifts, investor sentiment, or reactions to geopolitical events. Being able to analyze these changes helps investors stay ahead of potential market fluctuations.

2.4 Bull and Bear Markets

Bull markets are periods characterized by rising asset prices and widespread optimism among investors. During these times, market sentiment is generally positive, leading to increased investment activities and higher stock prices. Investors are often more willing to take risks, driven by the hope of substantial returns. The confidence in the market's upward trajectory can create a self-reinforcing loop where rising prices attract more buyers, further pushing prices up.

Understanding the dynamics of bull markets requires recognizing several key indicators. One primary sign is a consistent increase in stock prices over a period. This upward trend is usually accompanied by strong economic growth indicators such as low unemployment rates, increasing GDP, and robust corporate earnings. These factors combined signal a healthy economic environment that supports higher valuations for stocks and other assets.

For investors, identifying these signs early can present significant investment opportunities. By recognizing a bull market in its early stages, investors can position themselves to benefit from the upward momentum. However, it's crucial to remain mindful of investor psychology during these periods. Overconfidence and irrational exuberance can lead to hasty decisions and speculative bubbles. Staying informed and making evidence-based decisions can help investors navigate bull markets wisely and avoid potential pitfalls.

In contrast, bear markets represent periods of falling asset prices and pervasive pessimism among investors. During a bear market, stock prices typically decline by 20% or more from recent highs, and negative sentiment dominates investor behavior. Economic challenges such as rising unemployment, decreasing GDP, and declining corporate earnings contribute to the gloomy outlook, causing many to pull back from investing.

Recognizing the onset of a bear market involves monitoring various indicators. A prolonged drop in stock prices, coupled with weak economic data, signals a bearish trend. Other signs include reduced consumer spending, lowered business investments, and general economic uncertainty. By paying attention to these factors, investors can prepare themselves for potential downturns and make strategic adjustments to their portfolios.

Investors must develop strategies to protect their assets during bear markets. Asset allocation and defensive stock picks can play pivotal roles in minimizing losses. Diversifying investments across various sectors and asset classes can reduce risk exposure. Additionally, focusing on companies with solid fundamentals and stable earnings can provide a cushion against market volatility. By adopting a cautious and well-informed approach, investors can weather bear markets more effectively.

The implications of bull and bear markets extend beyond immediate asset price changes. For long-term investors, understanding these market cycles is crucial for building resilient investment strategies. Bull markets offer opportunities for growth and wealth accumulation, but they also require vigilance to avoid overexposure to riskier assets. Conversely, bear markets necessitate careful management to preserve capital and capitalize on recovery opportunities when the market rebounds.

Staying educated about market trends and maintaining a diversified portfolio are essential steps to navigate these cycles. Investors should consistently review their financial goals, risk tolerance, and investment time horizons to ensure alignment with current market conditions. By doing so, they can make informed decisions that support their long-term financial well-being.

2.5 Wrapping It Up

In this chapter, we've delved deep into the essential stock market terms, providing you with a solid foundation to begin your investment journey. We started by distinguishing between stocks and shares, emphasizing how these fundamental concepts are crucial for anyone planning to enter the stock market. Stocks represent ownership in a company and come with various benefits such as potential capital gains and voting rights. Shares, on the other hand, denote specific units of ownership within a given company, allowing investors to gauge their level of investment accurately.

Revisiting our discussion, we examined the differences between common and preferred stocks. These distinctions are critical because they guide your investment decisions based on your risk tolerance and income preferences. Common stocks might offer higher returns but come with variable dividends and voting rights, while preferred stocks provide fixed dividends at the expense of voting privileges.

We also explored the types of shares—authorized, issued, and outstanding—providing insights into a company's financial health and growth strategies. Understanding these can help you make informed decisions about where and how to allocate your funds wisely. For instance, a company with many authorized but unissued shares might be planning future financing rounds, signaling potential dilution of existing shares.

One thing that should concern some readers is the complexity of these terms and how they interact in real-world scenarios. It's easy to get overwhelmed by the jargon and nuances, but gaining familiarity with these concepts is indispensable for effective market navigation. The consequences of not understanding these terms can range from making uninformed investment choices to potentially facing significant financial losses. Proper knowledge empowers you to make strategic decisions that align with your financial goals and risk tolerance.

On a broader scale, being well-versed in stock market terminology enables more than just personal financial growth; it contributes to a more informed and engaged investor community. This collective awareness can lead to more stable and efficient markets, benefiting all participants by fostering a culture of informed decision-making and responsible investing.

As you continue your journey into the world of investments, remember that understanding these basic yet essential terms is only the beginning. The stock market is vast and ever-changing, requiring continuous learning and adaptation. Keep exploring, stay curious, and let your newfound knowledge guide you towards making smarter investment choices. Happy investing!

Chapter 3: Getting Started with Investing

Getting started with investing can feel like navigating a bewildering maze of financial jargon and complex choices. With so many options available, it's essential to have a clear plan to guide you through your investment journey. This chapter will simplify the process by laying out the foundational steps that every new investor needs to take. From defining your financial goals to creating a robust budget and understanding different investment types, you'll find practical advice tailored for those just beginning their venture into the stock market.

We'll dive into how setting clear financial goals can act as your compass, directing you toward smart investment decisions. You'll learn how to carve out a budget that not only meets your daily needs but also aligns with your long-term aspirations. We'll explore the importance of balancing short-term and long-term targets, along with aligning them with your risk tolerance and timeline. Additionally, we'll discuss the flexibility required to adapt your plans as life circumstances change. By the end of this chapter, you'll be equipped with actionable strategies and a solid roadmap to kickstart your investing journey with confidence.

3.1 Setting Financial Goals

Understanding the importance of setting financial goals is essential for guiding your investment decisions. Beginners often overlook this critical step, but it acts as a cornerstone for successful investing. Clear financial goals not only provide direction but also serve as a roadmap that influences every investment decision you make. Without them, it is easy to get lost in the myriad of investment options available.

Start by defining your objectives. This means taking a deep dive into what you want to achieve financially. Are you saving for retirement, a down payment on a house, or perhaps a child's education? Clearly outlining these goals gives you a solid foundation. It's important not to be vague. Specificity is key—know exactly what you're aiming for and when you want to achieve it. Writing down these objectives can also make them feel more real and attainable.

Creating a budget is the next crucial step. Budgeting helps you manage and allocate your funds effectively, ensuring that you have the resources necessary to meet your investment goals. Start by tracking your income and expenses meticulously. Identifying where your money goes each month will highlight areas where you can cut back and save more. Effective budgeting creates a healthy financial habit that supports both your daily needs and investment aspirations.

Establishing short-term and long-term targets is another vital practice. Short-term goals might include saving for a vacation or a small emergency fund, while long-term goals could involve retirement savings or purchasing a home. Aligning these targets with your risk tolerance and investment timeline allows you to create a balanced portfolio. For example, if you have a low risk tolerance and need the funds within five years, you might prefer safer investments like bonds over volatile stocks. Understanding your time frame and comfort with risk helps tailor your investment strategy to fit your unique needs.

Incorporate your investment goals into your budgeting plan. Allocate specific amounts towards different goals and stick to those allocations. For instance, set aside a portion of your monthly income expressly for your retirement fund, while another portion can go into a savings account for an emergency fund. This not only helps in reaching your goals systematically but also inculcates disciplined financial behavior.

Regularly reviewing and adjusting your goals is equally important. Financial circumstances change over time, and so should your objectives. Evaluate your progress periodically to see if you are on track. Life events such as a job change, marriage, or the birth of a child can significantly impact your financial situation. Thus, revisiting your goals ensures they remain relevant and achievable.

Modifying goals based on changing financial circumstances keeps your investment strategy flexible and resilient. You might need to allocate more funds to certain goals while pulling back from others. Documenting these changes and understanding their implications can help you stay on course and avoid any potential pitfalls.

By maintaining flexibility in your investment plans, you can better navigate financial uncertainties. Flexibility means being open to adjusting your strategies as needed, whether that involves reallocating assets, diversifying your portfolio, or even pausing certain investments temporarily. Adaptability is crucial for long-term financial health.

3.2 Choosing a Brokerage Account

In the realm of investing, selecting a brokerage account that aligns with your investment needs is crucial. This decision can significantly influence your overall investment experience and long-term financial goals. Let's delve into the steps you should consider to make an informed choice.

Researching Brokerage Options

Before choosing a brokerage account, it's essential to understand the different types available. Broadly speaking, there are two primary categories: full-service brokers and discount brokers. Full-service brokers provide a wide range of services, including investment advice, portfolio management, and retirement planning. These services come at a cost, often through higher fees or commission rates. Conversely, discount brokers offer minimal advisory services but provide a platform for executing trades at a lower cost. For beginners, discount brokers like Robinhood or Fidelity can be appealing due to their lower fees and user-friendly interfaces.

Furthermore, online reviews and comparisons can provide valuable insights into the strengths and weaknesses of various brokerages. Websites like Investopedia or Bogleheads.org can be helpful resources. They often feature user reviews, expert opinions, and detailed comparisons of brokerage features and fees. Paying attention to these reviews can help identify common issues or standout features that might align with your personal investment strategy.

Additionally, attending informational webinars or workshops hosted by brokerages can be beneficial. These events typically provide an overview of what the brokerage offers and how their platform works. Some brokerages even offer free trials or demo accounts, allowing potential customers to test the waters before committing. Taking advantage of these opportunities can give you hands-on experience and a better understanding of which brokerage suits your needs.

Evaluating Account Features

Once you have a list of potential brokerages, it's time to evaluate their account features. One critical aspect to consider is the availability of research tools and educational resources. Beginners will benefit significantly from access to comprehensive learning materials, such as tutorials, articles, and webinars. Brokerages like Fidelity and TD Ameritrade are known for their robust educational offerings, which can help you build your investment knowledge and confidence.

Another important feature is the range of investment products available. While most brokerages offer access to stocks, bonds, and ETFs (exchange-traded funds), some may also provide access to mutual funds, options, and cryptocurrencies. Depending on your investment goals, having a broader selection of products can provide greater flexibility and diversification opportunities.

Customer service and account security are also paramount. Reliable customer support can be a lifesaver when encountering technical issues or needing urgent assistance. Look for brokerages that offer multiple channels of support, including phone, email, and live chat. Additionally, ensure that the brokerage employs strong security measures, such as two-factor authentication and encryption, to protect your sensitive information and investments.

Comparing Costs

Cost is a significant factor in selecting a brokerage account. Different brokerages have varying fee structures, so it's essential to analyze these carefully. Common costs include commission fees for trades, account maintenance fees, and service charges for specific transactions. For instance, some brokerages might charge a commission per trade, while others offer commission-free trading but compensate through wider bid-ask spreads or other fees.

Account minimums are another consideration. Many brokerages require a minimum deposit to open an account, which can range from $0 to several thousand dollars. Ensure that the minimum required aligns with your initial investment budget. For example, if you're starting with a modest amount, brokers like Robinhood or Fidelity, which have no account minimums, might be more suitable.

It's also worth considering any hidden fees that might not be immediately apparent. These could include fees for inactivity, withdrawals, wire transfers, or even paper statements. A thorough review of the brokerage's fee schedule can prevent unexpected surprises and help you choose an account that won't erode your investment returns through excessive charges. Online resources and comparison tools can assist you in this analysis, providing a clearer picture of the total cost of ownership for each brokerage option.

Opening an Account

After identifying a brokerage that meets your needs in terms of features and costs, the next step is to open an account. Most brokerages have streamlined this process to be user-friendly and straightforward. Begin by visiting the brokerage's website or downloading their app, where you'll typically find an option to create a new account.

You will need to complete an application form with personal information, including your name, address, Social Security number, and employment details. Be prepared to answer questions about your financial situation and investment objectives, as these help the brokerage tailor their services to your profile. Once you've submitted the application, the brokerage will usually perform an identity verification check.

Funding your new brokerage account is the next step. Most brokerages offer multiple methods to deposit funds, such as bank transfers, wire transfers, or even checks. Follow the instructions provided by the brokerage to link your bank account and transfer money. It's advisable to start with an amount you're comfortable with, keeping in mind any account minimums and initial deposits required.

Finally, familiarize yourself with the brokerage's interface and features. Take some time to explore the dashboard, learn how to place trades, and utilize the research and educational tools available. Many brokerages offer tutorial videos or guided tours of their platform, which can be incredibly helpful for beginners. Understanding how to navigate the platform efficiently will enhance your trading experience and set you up for successful investing.

3.3 Understanding Different Types of Trading Accounts

Understanding the different types of trading accounts is an essential first step for anyone looking to start investing. Two common types of accounts used by investors are cash accounts and margin accounts. Each has distinct features that can significantly impact your investment strategy.

A cash account is straightforward: you can only invest the funds you have deposited in the account. This simplicity makes cash accounts a suitable choice for beginners who want to avoid overextending themselves financially. Since you're limited to the amount of money you actually have, there's less risk of accumulating debt. Typically, they are also easier to understand and manage, as you're using your own money without borrowing from the broker.

On the other hand, a margin account allows you to borrow money from your brokerage to purchase securities. This type of account can potentially amplify your gains because it provides access to more significant sums than you might have on hand. However, margin accounts come with risks, including the possibility of losing more money than you initially invested due to market fluctuations. Interest payments on borrowed funds also add cost elements that need to be managed carefully. For these reasons, understanding the mechanics and risks associated with margin accounts is crucial before diving in.

Next, let's explore retirement accounts, which offer tax advantages encouraging long-term investment plans. One popular option is the Individual Retirement Account (IRA), available in Traditional and Roth versions. Traditional IRAs allow you to contribute pre-tax income, reducing your taxable income for the year in which contributions are made. However, withdrawals in retirement are taxed as regular income. This setup benefits those who expect to be in a lower tax bracket upon retirement.

In contrast, Roth IRAs are funded with post-tax dollars, meaning there are no immediate tax deductions. The significant advantage here is that qualified withdrawals in retirement are entirely tax-free, making it beneficial if you expect to be in a higher tax bracket later. It's also worth noting employer-sponsored plans like 401(k)s, which often include employer matching contributions. These plans automatically deduct contributions from your paycheck, offering a disciplined approach to saving for retirement.

Specialized accounts cater to specific needs, providing flexibility for various investment scenarios. Custodial accounts, for instance, are designed for minors, allowing parents or guardians to manage investments on their behalf until they reach adulthood. These accounts can serve as excellent tools for teaching financial literacy and investing fundamentals to young people. They also enable parents to save and invest for their child's future expenses, such as education costs.

Health Savings Accounts (HSAs) are another example of specialized accounts, targeting healthcare expenses. HSAs provide triple tax advantages: contributions are tax-deductible, earnings grow tax-free, and withdrawals for qualified medical expenses are tax-free. This combination makes them a powerful tool for managing healthcare costs while investing for potential growth. For individuals with high-deductible health plans, HSAs offer a way to save and grow their money earmarked for future medical needs.

Lastly, consider the concept of paper trading as a low-risk way to begin investing. Paper trading involves simulated trading using virtual money rather than real capital. This practice allows new investors to experiment with different strategies and become comfortable with the trading platform's features before committing actual funds. It's a practical step to build confidence and develop skills without the fear of financial loss.

One significant benefit of paper trading is the opportunity to test and refine investment strategies in a risk-free environment. By engaging in simulated trades, you can track your performance and make adjustments based on real-time data. This process helps in identifying pitfalls and successful tactics, providing valuable insights that can improve future real-money trades. Moreover, many brokerages offer paper trading platforms, making it accessible for anyone interested in learning how to navigate the stock market effectively.

Another advantage is that paper trading helps you familiarize yourself with the market's volatility and behavioral patterns without the stress of losing actual money. This experience is invaluable, as it teaches restraint and prevents impulsive decisions during periods of market turbulence. As you developed trading discipline and methodological approaches, you will be better equipped to handle emotional aspects of investing when real money is at stake.

3.4 Basic Steps to Buy Your First Stock

Researching Stocks

When getting started with investing, the first crucial step is researching stocks. This involves conducting both fundamental and technical analysis to identify potential investments. Fundamental analysis entails evaluating a company's financial health by examining metrics such as cash flow, return on assets (ROA), and profit retention for future growth. By delving into a company's balance sheet, income statement, and cash flow statement, investors can form a comprehensive picture of the business's financial stability and growth prospects.

On the other hand, technical analysis focuses on studying stock price movements and trading volumes over time. Investors analyze stock charts and trends to determine the best times to buy or sell. This approach assumes that historical price movements and patterns are likely to repeat themselves. Tools like moving averages, trend lines, and volume analysis help investors predict future price actions and make informed decisions. Both fundamental and technical analyses offer insights that complement each other, providing a well-rounded view of a stock's potential for investment.

In addition to these analyses, keeping an eye on market news, industry developments, and economic indicators is essential. These external factors can significantly influence stock prices and should be part of your research process. Combining thorough research with ongoing learning will empower you to make informed and confident investment decisions. Remember, the goal is to identify undervalued stocks with strong growth potential.

Placing an Order

Once you've identified a stock worth purchasing, the next step is placing an order. This process begins with choosing the appropriate type of order. The most common types include market orders, limit orders, and stop orders. A market order buys or sells a stock at the current market price, ensuring quick execution but without control over the price. Limit orders, in contrast, allow you to specify the maximum price you're willing to pay or the minimum price you're willing to accept, offering more control but no guarantee of execution if the market doesn't reach your set price.

Next, you'll need to set the quantity of shares you wish to purchase and the price per share if you're using a limit order. It's vital to consider your budget and how much of your portfolio you want to allocate to a particular stock. Once you've decided, entering this information accurately on your brokerage platform is critical to ensure the trade is executed according to your wishes.

After placing the order, monitoring the trade execution is key. Ensure that the order has been fulfilled and review the confirmation details provided by your broker. If using a limit order, you may need to wait until your specified conditions are met. Keeping track of your orders and their statuses helps protect against errors and ensures that your investment strategy is implemented correctly.

Portfolio Management

Effective portfolio management is crucial for tracking and optimizing your investments. Strategies for monitoring your stock investments involve regularly reviewing your portfolio's performance. This includes assessing the performance of individual stocks and the portfolio as a whole relative to benchmarks like market indices. Regular evaluation helps you understand what's working and what isn't, enabling you to make necessary adjustments.

Diversification is another critical aspect of portfolio management. Spreading your investments across various sectors, industries, and asset classes can reduce risk. If one sector underperforms, the others may offset the losses, stabilizing your overall portfolio returns. Keeping a balanced mix of stocks helps manage risks associated with market volatility and unforeseen events.

Implementing a plan for regular portfolio review is essential. Set intervals—monthly, quarterly, or annually—to reassess your investments aligned with your financial goals and risk tolerance. During these reviews, consider rebalancing your portfolio to maintain your desired asset allocation. Rebalancing involves selling assets that have grown beyond your target proportion and buying those that now constitute a smaller portion of your portfolio. This disciplined approach ensures that your investments remain aligned with your long-term objectives.

Risk Management

Risk management is a fundamental aspect of investing, particularly for beginners who may not be familiar with the market's intricacies. One effective risk management strategy is setting stop-loss orders. A stop-loss order automatically sells a stock when it reaches a predetermined price, limiting potential losses. This tool protects your investments from significant downward spirals by providing a safety net that activates without requiring constant monitoring of market conditions.

Diversification is another key strategy to mitigate risk. By spreading your investments across different stocks, industries, and even asset classes, you can reduce the impact of any single investment's poor performance on your overall portfolio. Diversification acts as a buffer, helping to stabilize your returns and minimize exposure to sector-specific risks.

3.5 Wrapping It Up

In this chapter, we've walked through the foundational steps necessary for beginner investors to kick-start their journey in the stock market. We began by emphasizing the importance of setting clear financial goals, which serve as the cornerstone for any successful investment strategy. Understanding what you want to achieve financially allows you to create a roadmap that guides your decisions and keeps you focused amid the many investment options available.

We've discussed how defining specific objectives is crucial. Whether you're saving for retirement, a down payment on a house, or a child's education, having concrete goals provides stability and direction. Creating a budget helps ensure you allocate sufficient resources towards these goals. By tracking income and expenses, you can identify areas where you can save more and manage your funds effectively.

Aligning your short-term and long-term targets with your risk tolerance and investment timeline is essential for building a balanced portfolio. This alignment ensures that your investment choices are suitable for your unique needs and circumstances. Incorporating these goals into your budgeting plan supports disciplined financial behavior and systematic progress toward your objectives.

We also highlighted the necessity of regularly reviewing and adjusting your goals. Life events such as job changes, marriage, or the birth of a child can significantly alter your financial situation. Staying flexible and ready to modify your plans based on changing circumstances ensures that your investment strategy remains relevant and resilient.

Choosing the right brokerage account was another major focus. We explored the differences between full-service and discount brokers, giving you the tools to select an option that best fits your needs. Researching brokerage features, evaluating account options, and comparing costs help you make an informed choice. Opening an account becomes straightforward when you follow the outlined steps, setting you up for successful investing from the start.

Understanding the various types of trading accounts available allows you to make better decisions based on your investment goals. Cash accounts provide simplicity and reduce the risk of debt, while margin accounts offer opportunities for larger gains at higher risks. Retirement accounts like IRAs and 401(k)s provide tax advantages encouraging long-term savings. Specialized accounts, such as custodial accounts and HSAs, cater to specific needs and offer unique benefits.

Taking the first steps to buy stocks involves thorough research, effective order placement, and careful portfolio management. By conducting fundamental and technical analyses, you can identify promising stocks. Placing accurate orders and monitoring their execution ensures your investments align with your strategy. Managing your portfolio through regular reviews and diversification minimizes risk and maximizes returns.

Finally, risk management is a crucial aspect of investing. Setting stop-loss orders and diversifying your investments protect against significant losses and stabilize your returns. Paper trading offers a risk-free way to practice and refine your strategies before committing real money, helping you build confidence and experience.

As you move forward in your investment journey, remember that flexibility and continuous learning are key. The stock market is dynamic, and staying informed will empower you to adapt and succeed. With the foundational knowledge and practical steps covered in this chapter, you're well-equipped to take control of your financial future and build wealth through smart investing. Happy investing!

Chapter 4: Analyzing Stocks

Analyzing stocks is an essential skill for anyone looking to invest in the stock market. Before diving into investments, it's crucial to understand how to evaluate the viability of potential stocks. This chapter provides you with a comprehensive guide on various methods and tools needed to make informed investment decisions. Whether you're a working professional or a college student, mastering these techniques can significantly impact your financial future.

In this chapter, you'll learn about fundamental analysis, technical analysis, and how to read financial statements. We'll explore key financial ratios, including the Price-to-Earnings ratio and debt-to-equity ratio, that help determine a company's performance and stability. You'll also discover how to use stock screeners to filter and identify potential investment opportunities efficiently. By the end of this chapter, you'll be equipped with the knowledge to analyze stocks like a pro, making smarter and more strategic investment choices.

4.1 Fundamental Analysis

Understanding how fundamental analysis plays a crucial role in assessing the intrinsic value of a stock is essential for any investor. At its core, fundamental analysis aims to evaluate a company's overall health and potential for future growth by examining various financial statements and metrics. This method involves digging deep into a company's balance sheets, income statements, and cash flow statements, offering a comprehensive view of its financial position.

Analyzing these financial documents allows investors to gauge aspects such as revenue growth, profitability, and cash management. The balance sheet, for instance, provides insights into a company's assets, liabilities, and shareholders' equity at a particular point in time. By comparing these elements, one can determine the company's net worth and its ability to cover its obligations. On the other hand, the income statement focuses on revenue and expenses, highlighting how efficiently a company generates profit over a period. Lastly, the cash flow statement breaks down cash inflows and outflows from operating, investing, and financing activities, shedding light on a company's liquidity and cash handling capabilities.

Together, these statements offer a holistic view of a company's financial health. For example, a balance sheet with high levels of debt may signal financial instability, while an income statement showing consistent revenue growth can indicate a thriving business. Cash flow statements revealing robust operating cash flow suggest strong operational efficiency. Therefore, thorough analysis of these documents can guide investors in making informed decisions.

Key financial ratios play a significant role in evaluating the performance of a company. Ratios like the Price-to-Earnings (P/E) ratio, debt-to-equity ratio, and return on equity provide valuable benchmarks. The P/E ratio compares a company's current share price to its per-share earnings, helping investors assess whether a stock is overvalued or undervalued relative to its earnings. A lower P/E ratio might indicate an undervalued stock, whereas a higher ratio could suggest overvaluation.

The debt-to-equity ratio measures a company's financial leverage by comparing its total liabilities to shareholders' equity. A high ratio could mean that a company is heavily reliant on debt to finance its growth, which might be risky during economic downturns. Conversely, a low ratio indicates a more conservative approach to financing, often seen as less risky. Return on equity (ROE) evaluates how effectively management uses shareholders' equity to generate profit. A higher ROE signifies efficient use of investment funds, reflecting positively on the management's capability.

Monitoring these ratios enables investors to compare companies within the same industry, offering a clearer picture of relative performance. For instance, a company with a lower P/E ratio but higher ROE compared to its peers might be a more attractive investment. Similarly, a firm with a manageable debt-to-equity ratio can be considered financially stable, reducing the risk associated with excessive leverage.

In addition to financial ratios, examining a company's market share, competitive advantages, and growth prospects is vital. Market share indicates the company's portion of total sales in its industry, revealing its market dominance and competitive positioning. A growing market share suggests that the company is capturing more customers and possibly outperforming competitors.

Competitive advantages, such as unique products, cost leadership, or strong brand recognition, provide a company with an edge over rivals. These advantages can lead to sustained market share and long-term profitability. For example, a tech company with a patented innovation has a significant advantage over competitors lacking similar technology. Growth prospects involve evaluating future potential based on industry trends, demographic shifts, and the company's strategic initiatives. An expanding industry or favorable market conditions can propel a company's future growth.

By understanding these factors, investors can better assess the long-term viability of a stock. A company with a large market share, strong competitive advantages, and positive growth prospects is more likely to deliver sustained returns. Conversely, a firm struggling to maintain its market share or lacking differentiation may face challenges in achieving long-term success.

Assessing the management team's track record, strategic vision, and corporate governance practices is another critical aspect of fundamental analysis. Experienced and capable management is essential for steering the company toward its goals. Evaluating past performance can provide insights into the management's effectiveness in executing strategies and driving growth.

Strategic vision encompasses the management's plans for future growth, including product development, market expansion, and operational improvements. A clearly articulated and feasible strategic vision can instill confidence in investors regarding the company's future direction. Additionally, strong corporate governance practices ensure transparency, accountability, and adherence to ethical standards, mitigating risks associated with managerial misconduct or poor decision-making.

Effective management can significantly influence a company's performance and shareholder value. For instance, a leadership team with a history of successful turnarounds or innovative product launches demonstrates the ability to navigate challenges and capitalize on opportunities. Hence, assessing these attributes is key to determining whether a company is well-positioned for sustained growth.

Corporate governance practices are equally important in ensuring that a company's operations align with shareholder interests. Good governance includes having independent board members, transparent reporting, and policies that protect shareholder rights. Companies with robust governance structures are more likely to make sound decisions that contribute to long-term value creation. Poor governance, on the other hand, can lead to conflicts of interest, mismanagement, and ultimately harm the company's reputation and performance.

4.2 Technical Analysis

One of the most fascinating aspects of stock analysis is the use of historical price and volume data to forecast future stock movements through technical analysis. This method involves identifying patterns and trends on stock charts that may indicate potential price changes. By recognizing these patterns, investors can make informed decisions about when to buy or sell a stock.

A key approach in technical analysis is identifying chart patterns such as support and resistance levels, trendlines, and moving averages. Support levels represent points where a stock's price tends to stop falling, while resistance levels signify points where the price stops rising. Identifying these levels can be crucial for making trading decisions. For instance, if a stock consistently bounces off a particular support level, it might indicate a good entry point. Conversely, recognizing a strong resistance can signal an opportune moment to sell. Trendlines, which connect the highs or lows of a stock over a specific period, help investors determine the overall direction of the market, whether upward, downward, or sideways. Moving averages, which smooth out price data to create a single flowing line, highlight the average price movement over a set period and are instrumental in spotting long-term trends.

Furthermore, technical indicators such as the Relative Strength Index (RSI) and Moving Average Convergence Divergence (MACD) are essential tools in confirming trading signals and gauging market momentum. RSI measures the speed and change of price movements, indicating whether a stock is overbought or oversold. For instance, an RSI above 70 suggests that a stock might be overbought and due for a correction, while an RSI below 30 indicates it might be oversold and poised for a rebound. MACD, on the other hand, reveals changes in the strength, direction, momentum, and duration of a trend. It works by comparing short-term and long-term moving averages and can help traders spot potential buy and sell signals. When the MACD line crosses above the signal line, it often signals a buying opportunity, whereas a cross below the signal line can indicate a selling point.

Analyzing trading volume is another critical component of technical analysis. Volume, the number of shares traded during a given period, can provide insights into market sentiment and validate price trends. High trading volumes often accompany significant price movements, suggesting strong investor interest and potentially reinforcing the trend. For example, if a stock breaks through a resistance level with high volume, it is more likely to continue rising compared to a breakout with low volume. Conversely, if a price drop occurs on heavy volume, it could signal a genuine shift in market sentiment rather than a temporary dip. By scrutinizing volume patterns, investors can better understand the underlying forces driving price changes and make more confident trading decisions.

Effective risk management is another vital aspect of using technical analysis. Implementing stop-loss orders and setting risk-reward ratios based on technical signals helps protect investments and manage potential losses. A stop-loss order automatically sells a stock when it reaches a predefined price, minimizing the emotional decision-making component of trading. For instance, an investor might set a stop-loss order just below a support level to limit losses if the stock breaks downward. Setting appropriate risk-reward ratios also ensures that potential profits justify the risks taken. By analyzing technical indicators and market conditions, investors can determine optimal entry and exit points, maximizing gains while mitigating losses.

4.3 Reading Financial Statements

Developing the skill to interpret financial statements accurately is crucial for making informed investment decisions. Financial statements provide a detailed snapshot of a company's financial health, helping investors determine whether a stock is worth their money. By understanding these documents, working professionals and students can better navigate the complex world of stock investments.

The income statement is one of the most informative tools available. It outlines a company's revenue, expenses, and profitability over a specific period. Understanding these elements is essential for assessing a company's earnings potential. Revenue indicates how much a company makes from its core business activities, while expenses outline the costs incurred in generating that revenue. Profitability metrics such as net income and earnings per share help investors understand how efficiently a company turns revenue into profit.

To dive deeper, examine profitability trends. Assessing net income growth or decline over multiple quarters can reveal how well a company adapts to market conditions. Comparing data from various periods helps identify patterns, showing whether earnings are consistently improving or declining. This comparison also highlights seasonal impacts on the business, offering a clearer picture of financial performance throughout the year.

Additionally, comparing income statements with industry peers gives context. Metrics like gross margin, operating margin, and net profit margin offer insights into operational efficiency and profitability relative to competitors. Such comparisons help investors gauge a company's competitive standing and potential for long-term success.

Moving on to balance sheets, evaluating assets, liabilities, and equity is vital for gauging a company's financial position. Assets represent what the company owns, including cash, inventory, and property. Liabilities reflect what the company owes, such as loans and accounts payable. Equity represents shareholders' residual interest after liabilities are deducted from assets, indicating the company's net worth.

A thorough analysis of the balance sheet involves calculating liquidity ratios like the current ratio and quick ratio. These ratios measure a company's ability to cover short-term obligations, providing insights into its operational efficiency and financial stability. A high current ratio suggests strong liquidity, meaning the company can easily meet short-term debts. On the other hand, the quick ratio offers a more stringent measure by excluding inventory from current assets.

It's also important to consider solvency ratios, such as the debt-to-equity ratio. This metric indicates how much debt a company uses to finance its operations relative to shareholder equity. A higher ratio may signal that a company is over-leveraged, increasing financial risk. Conversely, a lower ratio suggests a more conservative approach to financing, potentially reducing risk and enhancing long-term sustainability.

Analyzing cash flow from operating, investing, and financing activities is another crucial aspect of evaluating a company's financial health. The cash flow statement reveals how well a company manages its cash, which is essential for meeting ongoing financial obligations. Cash flow from operating activities includes transactions directly related to producing goods or services, giving insights into the company's core business performance.

Cash flows from investing activities indicate how well a company allocates resources toward growth and expansion. This section includes purchases and sales of physical assets, investments in securities, and acquisitions or divestitures. Positive cash flow in this area suggests prudent investment strategies, contributing to long-term growth.

Lastly, cash flows from financing activities show how a company funds its operations through debt and equity. This includes issuing bonds, taking loans, repurchasing shares, and paying dividends. Analyzing this section helps investors understand the company's capital structure and financial strategy. For instance, frequent debt issuance might indicate reliance on borrowing, while consistent dividend payments could signal financial stability and shareholder confidence.

To further evaluate a company's ability to meet financial obligations, investors should identify liquidity and solvency ratios. Liquidity ratios, such as the current ratio and quick ratio, assess the company's capacity to cover short-term debts using its most liquid assets. These ratios provide immediate insights into the company's day-to-day financial health and operational efficiency.

Solvency ratios, such as the debt-to-equity ratio, focus on long-term financial stability. These ratios highlight the proportion of debt used to finance operations relative to equity, revealing potential risks associated with high leverage. Companies with higher solvency ratios may face challenges in sustaining long-term growth due to heavy debt burdens.

Another critical solvency ratio to consider is the interest coverage ratio, which measures a company's ability to pay interest on its debt. A higher ratio suggests that a company generates enough earnings to cover interest expenses comfortably, reducing the risk of default. Investors looking for stable, low-risk investments favor companies with strong interest coverage ratios, indicating robust financial health and sound risk management practices.

4.4 Using Stock Screeners

Leveraging stock screeners as tools to filter and identify potential investment opportunities is vital for making informed decisions. Stock screeners allow investors to sift through thousands of stocks using specific criteria to find the best fits for their portfolios. They essentially automate the preliminary research phase, enabling both seasoned and novice investors to streamline their decision-making process.

First, defining specific investment criteria is crucial in using stock screeners effectively. Investors should start by setting parameters like industry sector, which helps in narrowing down companies operating within a particular market. Focusing on sectors that align with an investor's knowledge or interest can increase the likelihood of identifying promising investments. For instance, an investor keen on technology might filter for tech companies exclusively, ensuring the results are relevant.

Market capitalization (market cap) is another essential criterion. It represents the total market value of a company's outstanding shares and indicates its size. Screening stocks by market cap allows investors to target large-cap, mid-cap, or small-cap companies based on their risk tolerance and investment goals. Large-cap stocks are usually considered safer but offer slower growth, while small caps might present higher growth potential but come with increased risk.

Financial ratios serve as critical indicators of a company's health and performance. Ratios such as the price-to-earnings (P/E) ratio, debt-to-equity ratio, and return on equity (ROE) provide insight into valuation, financial stability, and profitability. By incorporating these ratios into screening criteria, investors can identify companies that meet specific financial benchmarks, ensuring a more refined and objective selection process.

Customizing filters to match individual investment preferences and risk tolerance enhances the usefulness of stock screeners. Every investor has unique goals and risk appetites; thus, it's important to adjust screener settings accordingly. For example, a conservative investor might prioritize low-volatility stocks with strong dividend yields, while a more aggressive investor could look for high-growth stocks with significant earnings momentum.

The ability to customize screening parameters means investors can set up complex queries that reflect their personal investment strategies. For instance, an investor could combine filters like low P/E ratio, high ROE, and minimal debt, aligning the results closely with their preference for undervalued yet profitable companies with strong balance sheets. This personalization ensures that the screened stocks are highly pertinent to the investor's goals, increasing the chances of successful investments.

Moreover, advanced screeners often offer no-code solutions for customization, making it accessible even for those without technical expertise. These tools allow users to create detailed filters intuitively through simple interfaces, so anyone can tailor screener functions without needing programming skills. This democratizes sophisticated market analysis, enabling more people to make informed investment choices.

Reviewing screened stock lists is a critical step after applying the initial filters. This involves conducting further research and due diligence on the shortlisted stocks to validate their potential. Investors should delve deeper into each company's fundamentals, including recent financial statements, management quality, and competitive positioning. This thorough examination helps confirm if the stocks meet all necessary investment criteria and align with one's strategic vision.

Part of this review process involves assessing key fundamental indicators such as earnings growth, revenue trends, and profit margins. Additionally, investors should examine qualitative factors like company news, industry developments, and potential regulatory impacts. Understanding the broader context in which these companies operate provides a more comprehensive view of their future prospects.

Comparing screened stocks against each other is also essential. Even after filtering and reviewing, investors often end up with multiple viable options. At this stage, it's useful to rank these stocks based on their overall attractiveness, considering both quantitative metrics and qualitative insights. This comparison helps narrow down to the most suitable candidates for investment, ensuring that the final selections are well-informed and strategically sound.

Establishing a routine for periodic screening is important for staying updated on new market opportunities. The stock market is dynamic, with conditions changing frequently due to economic shifts, company developments, and global events. Regularly revisiting and updating screening processes allows investors to keep track of emerging opportunities that fit their evolving criteria and risk profiles.

Incorporating new investment criteria based on market changes can lead to discovering different kinds of opportunities. For example, during economic downturns, investors might prioritize defensive sectors like utilities or healthcare, known for their resilience. Conversely, in a bull market, they might focus on high-growth sectors to maximize returns. Being adaptable with screening criteria helps investors stay nimble and responsive to market dynamics.

Refining screening strategies over time is crucial for long-term investment success. Investors should periodically analyze the effectiveness of their screeners and make adjustments as needed. This continuous improvement approach ensures that the screening process evolves with market conditions and personal investment goals. By doing so, investors can maintain a robust portfolio that aligns with their strategic objectives, maximizing the potential for growth and minimizing risks.

4.5 Wrapping It Up

In this chapter, we've delved into the essentials of evaluating stocks before making any investment decisions. By exploring fundamental analysis, technical analysis, reading financial statements, and using stock screeners, we've covered a comprehensive range of methods and tools to help you assess the viability of potential stock market investments.

Fundamental analysis is all about understanding the intrinsic value of a stock by examining a company's financial health and growth potential. We've looked at how analyzing balance sheets, income statements, and cash flow statements can give you a complete picture of a company's financial position. Additionally, financial ratios like the Price-to-Earnings (P/E) ratio, debt-to-equity ratio, and return on equity offer valuable benchmarks for comparing companies within the same industry.

We also discussed technical analysis, which uses historical price and volume data to predict future stock movements. Chart patterns, trendlines, and moving averages are key tools in this approach, along with indicators like the Relative Strength Index (RSI) and Moving Average Convergence Divergence (MACD), which help confirm trading signals and gauge market momentum. Analyzing trading volume and implementing risk management strategies further support making informed trading decisions.

Reading financial statements accurately is another critical skill we've emphasized. An income statement provides insights into a company's revenue, expenses, and profitability. A balance sheet shows its assets, liabilities, and equity, while a cash flow statement reveals how well the company manages its cash. Understanding these documents helps you make more informed investment choices, highlighting both immediate financial health and long-term sustainability.

Using stock screeners allows you to filter through thousands of stocks based on specific criteria, streamlining your decision-making process. Defining parameters like industry sector, market capitalization, and financial ratios can narrow down your options to the most promising investments. Customizing filters to match your investment preferences and conducting thorough research on shortlisted stocks ensures your selections align with your strategic goals.

As we return to our initial focus on evaluating stocks before investing, it's clear that utilizing a combination of these methods provides a well-rounded approach. However, it's important to recognize that no single method guarantees success. Each has its strengths and weaknesses, and it's the integration of multiple approaches that offers the best chance of making smart investment decisions.

Some readers might be concerned about the complexity involved in mastering these various techniques. It's true that learning to evaluate stocks can feel overwhelming, especially for beginners. But remember, investment knowledge builds over time with practice and continuous learning. Being patient with yourself as you develop these skills will pay off in the long run.

On a broader scale, understanding how to properly evaluate stocks empowers you to make more confident and informed investment decisions. This not only enhances your personal financial growth but also contributes to a more knowledgeable and resilient investor community. As more individuals become adept at evaluating stocks, the overall market becomes more efficient and stable.

So, as you move forward on your investment journey, keep honing your skills, stay curious, and be open to learning new things. The ability to evaluate stocks effectively is a powerful tool in building wealth and achieving financial security. Remember, every successful investor started where you are now, and with dedication and persistence, you too can become proficient in navigating the stock market.

Chapter 5: Building Your Portfolio

Building your portfolio involves understanding the importance of diversification and strategic asset allocation. This chapter delves into the methods and approaches that can help you create a balanced and diversified investment portfolio, crucial for long-term success in the stock market. Diversification spreads your investments across different assets, reducing the risk associated with any single investment. By diversifying, you can manage potential losses more effectively and enhance your overall returns.

In this chapter, you'll explore various asset allocation models, including Strategic Asset Allocation, Tactical Asset Allocation, and Dynamic Asset Allocation. Each strategy offers unique benefits and requires different levels of expertise and monitoring. You'll also learn about the significance of periodic rebalancing to maintain your desired risk level and ensure your portfolio remains aligned with your financial goals. Additionally, the discussion will cover sector rotation strategies and how global exposure can further diversify your investments, tapping into growth opportunities worldwide. With practical examples and insights, this chapter aims to equip you with essential tools and knowledge to build a robust and resilient investment portfolio.

5.1 Importance of Diversification

Diversification is a foundational strategy in investing, primarily because it helps in managing and mitigating risk. The principle of diversification lies in spreading investments across various assets, which ensures that the risk associated with any single investment is minimized. This approach can safeguard your portfolio from experiencing substantial losses if one particular asset underperforms.

For instance, let's take the 2008 financial crisis. Investors who had all their funds invested in real estate experienced massive losses. However, those who diversified their portfolios with bonds, stocks from different industries, and perhaps even commodities managed to cushion the blow. Diversification does not eliminate risk but distributes it more evenly, making it less likely for an entire portfolio to suffer catastrophic losses simultaneously. This is why financial advisors often emphasize that a well-diversified portfolio is a cornerstone of sound investment planning.

Not only does diversification help manage risk, but it also aids in enhancing returns. By allocating investments across different asset classes such as stocks, bonds, real estate, and commodities, investors can tap into multiple sources of potential profit. Each asset class reacts differently to market conditions. For example, when stock markets are down, bond prices often go up, providing a buffer against stock market losses. Similarly, while one industry may be facing a downturn, another might be flourishing, thus stabilizing overall returns.

A practical example can illustrate this: suppose you invest in technology stocks, healthcare stocks, and government bonds. If the tech sector faces regulatory hurdles, potentially causing stock prices to drop, your investments in the healthcare sector and government bonds may not be as heavily affected. As a result, the overall volatility of your portfolio is minimized, leading to a more stable return. This balance between high-risk and low-risk assets helps in achieving better risk-adjusted returns.

Another advantage of diversification is increased market exposure. Being diversified means having a stake in various market trends, which can be incredibly beneficial. Markets are cyclical and tend to favor different sectors at different times. For instance, during economic expansion phases, growth stocks tend to perform well, while in recessionary periods, defensive stocks and bonds become more attractive.

By being exposed to a variety of these market segments, an investor can benefit from growth opportunities across different cycles. Imagine missing out on a booming sector just because your investments were concentrated elsewhere. Diversifying ensures that you capture a wide array of growth opportunities, allowing your portfolio to benefit from positive movements in different parts of the market. In essence, diversification keeps you in the game, regardless of what sector or industry is currently performing well.

Lastly, understanding asset correlation is crucial in forming effective diversification strategies. Correlation measures how different assets move in relation to one another. Assets with low or negative correlations make for ideal diversification because their performances do not move in tandem. For example, historically, stocks and bonds tend to have a low correlation. When stock prices fall, bond prices often rise, helping to stabilize a diversified portfolio.

However, it's essential to recognize that not all assets will always behave predictably. During extreme market conditions, correlations can change. Therefore, ongoing assessment and rebalancing of your portfolio is necessary to maintain an optimal mix of assets. Diversification is not a one-time task but a continuous process of evaluating and adjusting.

5.2 Asset Allocation Strategies

When constructing a well-balanced portfolio, understanding different asset allocation models is crucial. The first model to discuss is Strategic Asset Allocation. This approach involves setting target percentages for various asset classes—such as stocks, bonds, and other investments—based on your financial goals, risk tolerance, and investment horizon. For example, a young professional with a longer time frame might allocate a higher percentage to stocks for growth potential, while someone nearing retirement may prefer a more conservative mix with greater emphasis on bonds.

A key guideline for Strategic Asset Allocation is to start by assessing your risk tolerance. Are you comfortable with market volatility, or do you prefer stability? Your answer will influence the proportion of assets in your portfolio. Next, align these proportions with your long-term financial objectives. This structured approach minimizes emotional decision-making, helping you stick to your plan during market fluctuations. Regularly reviewing and adjusting your allocations ensures they remain aligned with your evolving needs and market conditions.

Implementing Strategic Asset Allocation requires discipline and consistency. Once you've set your targets, periodic rebalancing becomes essential. If one asset class performs exceptionally well, it might skew your original allocation, resulting in unintended risk exposure. By rebalancing, you can bring your portfolio back to its intended balance, maintaining the risk-return profile suitable for your goals and ensuring long-term stability and performance.

Moving on, Tactical Asset Allocation allows for more flexibility. This strategy enables investors to adjust their asset mix in response to short-term market opportunities or risks. Unlike the strategic approach, which focuses on long-term targets, tactical allocation involves making temporary adjustments to take advantage of favorable conditions or to mitigate potential losses.

For those new to investing, it's important to note that Tactical Asset Allocation requires active monitoring and a solid understanding of market trends. While this method can enhance returns, it also carries increased risk if not executed properly. Short-term market movements can be unpredictable, and frequent trading can lead to higher transaction costs and potential tax implications. Therefore, it's generally recommended for more experienced investors or those working with a financial advisor.

To successfully employ Tactical Asset Allocation, consider keeping a portion of your portfolio flexible. This means having a clear baseline (your strategic allocation) but being ready to shift a percentage of assets based on current market analysis. For instance, if economic indicators suggest an upcoming boom in technology, you might temporarily increase your allocation in tech stocks. However, always ensure these shifts are grounded in sound research and aligned with your overall investment strategy to avoid unnecessary risks.

Dynamic Asset Allocation takes another step by continuously adjusting your portfolio based on changing economic conditions and updated investment outlooks. This proactive approach recognizes that markets and personal circumstances evolve, necessitating ongoing vigilance and adaptation. Instead of committing to fixed targets like in strategic allocation, dynamic allocation remains fluid and responsive.

One of the main advantages of Dynamic Asset Allocation is its adaptability. Investors can respond more readily to economic signals, such as interest rate changes, inflation trends, or GDP growth rates. This responsiveness can potentially yield higher returns than static strategies, especially in volatile markets. However, it demands a high level of expertise and time commitment. Constant monitoring of economic indicators and market forecasts is crucial for making informed adjustments.

To implement a Dynamic Asset Allocation strategy effectively, consider setting up a framework that incorporates regular reviews and predefined criteria for shifting allocations. For example, if inflation rises above a certain threshold, you might reduce bond holdings and increase investments in commodities or real estate. This structured yet flexible approach ensures that adjustments are systematic rather than impulsive, balancing the need for responsiveness with the principles of disciplined investing.

Lastly, exploring Alternative Asset Allocation provides a broader perspective on creating a diversified portfolio. This model includes unconventional assets such as real estate, commodities, or even private equity. These asset classes can offer diversifying benefits beyond traditional stocks and bonds, often behaving differently under various market conditions, which can help stabilize your portfolio's performance.

Real estate, for instance, can provide steady income through rental yields and potential capital appreciation. On the other hand, commodities like gold or oil often serve as hedges against inflation and currency fluctuations. However, investing in alternative assets can be complex, with unique risks and liquidity considerations. It's essential to conduct thorough research or seek expert advice before including them in your portfolio.

5.3 Rebalancing Your Portfolio

One of the key strategies in portfolio management is periodic rebalancing. Market fluctuations can significantly impact your investment mix, altering the proportions and potentially exposing you to more risk than intended. For instance, if stocks outperform bonds consistently over a period, the equity portion of your portfolio might grow beyond its original target allocation. This imbalance can increase your overall risk since equities generally carry higher volatility compared to bonds or cash. Restoring the original proportions by selling some gains from stocks and reinvesting in bonds or other asset classes helps maintain the desired risk level.

Understanding how market performance impacts your asset allocation is crucial. During market downturns, certain investments may lose value faster than others. This disproportionate loss can tilt your portfolio away from its balanced state, with safer assets like bonds occupying a larger share inadvertently. Conversely, in a bull market, high-risk assets might swell, skewing the balance. Regular rebalancing ensures your investment strategy remains consistent with your financial goals and risk tolerance.

Ignoring market-induced imbalances can lead to unintended investment risks. For instance, an overweight in equities during a market peak might result in significant losses during a correction. By periodically reviewing and adjusting your allocations, you can mitigate the chances of such setbacks, ensuring a more stable growth trajectory for your portfolio. Rebalancing acts as a safeguard against market uncertainties, preserving the strategic integrity of your investment plan.

Different approaches to rebalancing cater to varying investor needs and preferences. Time-based rebalancing is a common approach where adjustments are made at set intervals, such as annually or semi-annually. This method offers simplicity and consistency, making it easier to adhere to a disciplined investment strategy. However, it might not always align perfectly with market movements, possibly leading to missed opportunities or unnecessary transactions.

Threshold-based rebalancing offers a more dynamic approach by making adjustments only when asset class weights deviate from their targets by a predetermined percentage. This method allows for rebalancing actions that reflect actual changes in market conditions rather than arbitrary timeframes. While this can be more efficient, it requires vigilant monitoring of your portfolio and a clear understanding of acceptable deviation thresholds.

Combining both methods can also be effective. For instance, you might set regular review dates to assess your portfolio but execute rebalancing only if deviations surpass specific thresholds. This hybrid approach balances the benefits of both strategies, ensuring timely adjustments without excessive trading. Ultimately, choosing a rebalancing method depends on your investment goals, risk tolerance, and the amount of time you can dedicate to managing your portfolio.

Tax considerations play a significant role when rebalancing, particularly for taxable accounts. Selling appreciated assets to rebalance can trigger capital gains taxes, which can erode your investment returns. It's essential to evaluate the tax implications before making any rebalancing decisions to minimize potential liabilities. Tax-efficient strategies, such as offsetting gains with losses elsewhere in your portfolio, can help manage these impacts.

In some cases, rebalancing within tax-advantaged accounts like IRAs or 401(k)s can be more beneficial since it doesn't incur immediate tax consequences. Another strategy is using dividends and interest payments to buy underweighted assets rather than selling overperforming ones. Consulting with a tax advisor can provide personalized guidance on incorporating tax strategies into your rebalancing efforts, optimizing your after-tax returns.

Additionally, long-term investors might consider utilizing tax-loss harvesting, which involves selling underperforming assets at a loss to offset taxable gains elsewhere. This approach can enhance tax efficiency while maintaining the desired asset allocation. Careful planning and awareness of tax rules can turn rebalancing into a powerful tool for maximizing net investment gains.

Establishing a systematic review schedule for your portfolio is vital to ensure continuous alignment with your financial goals. A regular review, whether quarterly, semi-annually, or annually, allows you to monitor performance, adjust for life changes, and stay informed about market trends. This practice ensures that your portfolio remains responsive to both personal circumstances and external economic conditions.

During each review, assess not just the asset allocation but also each individual investment's performance relative to your expectations and benchmarks. This comprehensive evaluation can highlight areas needing attention, whether it's replacing underperforming funds or reconsidering the suitability of certain asset classes in light of evolving market dynamics.

Moreover, sticking to a predefined review schedule fosters

discipline in your investment process. It prevents emotional decision-making driven by short-term market movements, promoting a long-term perspective essential for achieving financial success. Consistent reviews coupled with timely rebalancing reinforce your commitment to maintaining a well-balanced and goal-oriented portfolio.

5.4 Selecting Different Sectors and Industries

Diversifying your investment portfolio across various sectors and industries is a key strategy for capturing growth opportunities and mitigating sector-specific risks. Understanding industry performance can significantly enhance this approach. Sector rotation strategies, which involve moving investments between different sectors based on market cycles and trends, can help investors capitalize on the strengths of each sector at different times. For instance, when technology companies show rapid innovation and profit growth, channeling more investments into this sector could yield high returns.

Furthermore, historical data shows that certain sectors perform better during specific phases of economic cycles. For example, consumer staples tend to do well during economic downturns because people continue to need essential goods, while cyclical sectors like luxury goods might struggle. By staying informed about these trends, investors can strategically rotate their investments, ensuring they are well-positioned to take advantage of favorable conditions in each sector. This method not only maximizes returns but also reduces reliance on any single sector's performance.

Guidelines for implementing sector rotation should include regular monitoring of economic indicators and market trends to anticipate shifts. Investors should set up a systematic review process to evaluate sector performance regularly. Tools such as performance charts, economic forecasts, and expert analyses can be invaluable. This proactive approach allows investors to adjust their portfolios dynamically, ensuring ongoing alignment with market conditions.

Risk management is another critical benefit of diversifying across multiple industries. Investing solely in one sector increases vulnerability to downturns within that sector. However, spreading investments across varied industries minimizes potential losses if one sector underperforms. For example, if an investor's portfolio is concentrated in the energy sector and there's a significant drop in oil prices, the entire portfolio could suffer severe losses.

By contrast, a diversified portfolio might include investments in the healthcare, technology, and consumer goods sectors, which may not be affected similarly by changes in oil prices. In this way, diversification acts as a buffer against market volatility, helping to stabilize overall portfolio performance. Additionally, it mitigates risks associated with industry-specific issues such as regulatory changes, technological disruptions, or competitive pressures, which can adversely affect individual sectors.

To effectively manage risk through diversification, investors should establish clear guidelines for sector allocation within their portfolios. These guidelines might include setting maximum exposure limits for any single sector and periodically reviewing allocations to ensure they remain balanced. It's also prudent to keep abreast of industry news and reports that may signal emerging risks or opportunities, enabling timely portfolio adjustments.

Global exposure is an aspect of diversification that provides access to growth opportunities outside domestic markets. Investing in diverse sectors globally allows investors to benefit from varying economic conditions and growth rates across countries. For instance, while the US technology sector might be booming, there could simultaneously be lucrative opportunities in emerging markets' industrial sectors.

This global diversification not only increases potential returns but also spreads risk over different geographical areas. Economic events affecting one region might not have the same impact elsewhere, thereby cushioning the overall portfolio against region-specific downturns. Moreover, some international sectors may offer unique growth prospects unavailable in domestic markets, further enriching the portfolio's performance.

Guidelines for achieving global exposure include researching and selecting sectors that show strong performance in various regions. Investors should consider using global index funds or exchange-traded funds (ETFs) to gain broad exposure to international markets, easing the complexity of managing individual stocks. Regularly reviewing geopolitical developments and economic reports from different countries can also help in making informed decisions about where to allocate resources.

Research and analysis play fundamental roles in identifying

promising sectors for investment. Thorough research involves evaluating sector trends, financial health of companies within those sectors, and broader economic indicators. Detailed analysis helps investors understand factors driving growth or posing risks, such as technological advancements, regulatory environments, and market demands.

For instance, analyzing demographic trends might reveal growing demand in the healthcare sector due to an aging population, suggesting it's a wise area for investment. Conversely, recognizing potential regulatory changes could highlight risks in sectors like fossil fuel energy, guiding investors to shift focus to more sustainable energy options.

Investors should follow several guidelines to ensure thorough research and analysis. They should utilize multiple sources of information, including financial news, sector reports, and expert opinions. Using analytical tools like SWOT (Strengths, Weaknesses, Opportunities, Threats) analysis can also provide deeper insights. Additionally, maintaining a systematic approach to track and review sector performance over time helps in making data-driven decisions that align with investment goals.

5.5 Wrapping It Up

In this chapter, we've delved into the essential strategies for crafting a diversified and balanced portfolio. We've emphasized how diversification mitigates risks by spreading investments across various assets. By doing so, investors are better protected against significant losses, as no single asset will overwhelmingly impact the entire portfolio. The 2008 financial crisis serves as a stark reminder of the necessity of diversification, highlighting how those with varied investments fared better during turbulent times.

We've also explored the benefits of diversification in enhancing returns. Allocating funds across different asset classes like stocks, bonds, real estate, and commodities can lead to more stable and potentially higher returns. Each asset class reacts differently to market conditions, providing a buffer against downturns in specific sectors. For example, while tech stocks might face regulatory challenges, healthcare stocks and bonds could help stabilize your portfolio.

Another crucial point discussed is understanding asset correlation. Low or negative correlations between assets mean they don't move in tandem, which is ideal for diversification. For instance, when stock prices fall, bond prices often rise, balancing the overall performance of a diversified portfolio. However, it's important to remember that correlations can change during extreme market conditions, necessitating regular assessment and adjustments to maintain an optimal mix.

When it comes to asset allocation, we covered three main strategies: Strategic, Tactical, and Dynamic Asset Allocation. Strategic Asset Allocation involves setting long-term targets based on your risk tolerance and financial goals. It's about maintaining these proportions through regular rebalancing. Tactical Asset Allocation, on the other hand, allows for short-term adjustments based on market conditions, offering flexibility but requiring active monitoring. Dynamic Asset Allocation continuously adjusts based on economic changes, demanding a high level of expertise and vigilance.

Rebalancing plays a vital role in managing your portfolio. Over time, market fluctuations can skew your initial allocation, exposing you to unintended risks. Regular rebalancing helps restore your desired proportions, ensuring consistency with your investment strategy. We discussed various rebalancing methods, including time-based and threshold-based approaches, each catering to different needs. Tax considerations and efficient strategies like tax-loss harvesting are also critical aspects of the rebalancing process.

Diversification goes beyond just asset classes; it extends to sectors and industries. Investing across various sectors ensures you capture growth opportunities while mitigating sector-specific risks. Understanding industry performance and implementing sector rotation strategies can help maximize returns. Historical data shows that sectors perform differently during economic cycles, allowing informed investors to position themselves advantageously.

Global exposure adds another layer of diversification, providing access to growth opportunities outside domestic markets. Diversifying internationally spreads risk across different regions, enhancing portfolio stability. Research and analysis are fundamental in identifying promising sectors and making informed investment decisions. Thorough research helps understand trends, risks, and opportunities, guiding you to allocate resources wisely.

As you consider these strategies, remember that investing is a continuous journey. It's essential to stay informed, regularly review your portfolio, and make adjustments as needed. Diversification is not a one-time task but an ongoing process that evolves with your financial goals and market conditions. Embrace the principles discussed in this chapter, and you'll be well on your way to building a robust, diversified portfolio capable of withstanding market fluctuations and achieving long-term investment success.

Chapter 6: Investment Strategies

Investing in the stock market offers a variety of strategies that cater to different financial goals and risk tolerance levels. From holding onto stocks for several years to making quick trades within days, the approach you choose significantly impacts your investment returns and experiences. Understanding these varying strategies can help align your investment activities with your personal financial objectives, whether you are saving for retirement, a significant purchase, or simply looking to grow your wealth.

This chapter delves into the nuances of long-term versus short-term investing, highlighting the benefits and risks associated with each method. You will also learn about growth investing techniques, where investors focus on companies with high potential for expansion and revenue increases. Additionally, the concept of value investing will be explored, which involves identifying undervalued stocks with solid fundamentals. Finally, we will discuss dividend investing, a strategy that focuses on generating regular income from reliable dividend-paying stocks. By the end of this chapter, you will have a comprehensive understanding of these diverse investment approaches, empowering you to make informed decisions that best suit your financial situation and goals.

6.1 Long-Term vs Short-Term Investing

Understanding the differences between long-term and short-term investing is crucial for aligning with your individual financial goals. Each approach has distinct characteristics, benefits, and risks suited to different needs and objectives. By exploring these differences, you can make informed decisions that fit your unique financial situation.

Long-term investing primarily involves holding investments for an extended period, typically five years or more. The primary advantage of this strategy is the ability to benefit from compounding growth, where earnings on investments are reinvested to generate additional earnings over time. This compounding effect can significantly increase the value of your investment portfolio, especially when combined with consistent contributions. For example, investing in a diversified mix of stocks and bonds can provide steady returns and grow your wealth substantially over several decades.

Additionally, long-term investing allows investors to take advantage of market trends and economic cycles. Stock markets tend to experience fluctuations in the short term, but over long periods, they historically trend upward. By staying invested through various market conditions, long-term investors can smooth out the volatility and potentially achieve higher returns. For instance, someone who invested in a broad stock index fund during a market downturn but held onto their investment for 20 years likely saw significant gains as the market recovered and grew.

Another critical aspect of long-term investing is its alignment with larger financial goals such as retirement planning, buying a home, or funding education expenses. These goals generally have extended timelines, making them well-suited for investments that appreciate over time. Compounded returns from long-term investments can help build a robust financial foundation, ensuring that you have the necessary funds when you reach your goals.

In contrast, short-term investing involves buying and selling securities within a relatively brief timeframe, often less than a year. The primary goal is to capitalize on market fluctuations to achieve quick gains. Short-term investors actively monitor market trends, economic news, and company performance to make timely buy and sell decisions. For example, purchasing stocks before a company's anticipated strong earnings report and selling them shortly after the announcement can yield immediate profits.

One of the main attractions of short-term investing is its potential for rapid returns. Unlike long-term strategies, which may take years to realize significant gains, short-term investments can deliver profits within months or even weeks. This makes it appealing for individuals looking to increase their income quickly or manage their cash flow more effectively. For instance, traders might use technical analysis to identify short-term price patterns and execute trades to exploit these movements.

However, short-term investing also comes with higher risks,

including increased exposure to market volatility. Prices of stocks and other securities can be highly unpredictable in the short run, leading to potential losses if prices move against an investor's expectations. Additionally, frequent trading activities can incur higher transaction costs and taxes, which may eat into overall profits. It's essential for short-term investors to have a clear strategy, remain disciplined, and stay informed about market dynamics.

Long-term investors can withstand market volatility and are less affected by short-term fluctuations. Market corrections and temporary declines are inherent parts of the market cycle, but long-term investors typically remain unfazed by these short-term movements. Their focus is on the long-term trajectory of their investments rather than daily price changes. This perspective helps in avoiding panic selling and staying committed to their investment strategy.

Patience is a virtue for long-term investors. They understand that building wealth through investing is a marathon, not a sprint. During periods of market turbulence, long-term investors maintain composure and view these times as opportunities to purchase quality investments at discounted prices. This disciplined approach contributes to more stable and sustainable growth of their portfolios over time. For instance, consistently investing in a low-cost index fund regardless of market conditions can result in impressive returns after several decades.

Moreover, long-term investing aligns with a "buy and hold" philosophy, minimizing the need for constant monitoring and adjustment of investment positions. This strategy reduces emotional decision-making driven by short-term market movements and helps in maintaining a coherent investment plan. Investors can set their financial goals, develop an investment plan, and periodically review their progress without getting swayed by market noise. This long-term focus is particularly beneficial for those with busy schedules who prefer a hands-off approach to managing their investments.

On the other hand, short-term investing is suitable for achieving quick gains or managing cash flow. For individuals needing liquidity or expecting near-term expenses, short-term investments offer the flexibility to access funds relatively quickly. The ability to convert investments into cash on short notice provides confidence and peace of mind, especially in emergencies or unforeseen financial situations. For instance, setting aside funds in short-term bonds or high-yield savings accounts can ensure readily available resources when needed.

The dynamic nature of short-term investing requires a proactive approach to seize opportunities as they arise. Traders utilize various strategies, such as day trading, swing trading, or arbitrage, to profit from short-term price movements. These techniques demand staying up-to-date with market developments, analyzing charts, and reacting swiftly to changing conditions. While engaging, this active management style necessitates a higher level of attention and involvement compared to long-term investing.

However, the fast-paced nature of short-term investing also demands a cautious attitude towards risk management. Implementing stop-loss orders, diversifying holdings, and setting precise trade entry and exit points are essential practices to protect capital and mitigate potential losses. Investors should conduct thorough research and maintain a disciplined approach to avoid impulsive decisions driven by emotions or market hype. Trading platforms and tools can assist in monitoring positions and executing trades efficiently, aiding short-term investors in their pursuit of gains.

6.2 Growth Investing

Growth investing is a strategy that focuses on capital appreciation by targeting companies with strong growth prospects. These companies are often characterized by rapid revenue and earnings growth, which can translate into significant returns for investors. Growth investors typically look for businesses that have innovative products or services, expanding market shares, or robust business models that set them apart from their competitors. By investing in such companies, individuals can potentially see their investments grow substantially over time.

One of the key components of growth investing is research and analysis. Identifying promising growth stocks requires a deep understanding of a company's financial health, competitive advantages, and market potential. Investors need to analyze financial statements, including income statements, balance sheets, and cash flow statements, to gauge the company's performance and future potential. Additionally, keeping up with industry trends, news, and economic factors can provide valuable insights into whether a company is poised for growth. This thorough analysis helps investors make informed decisions about which stocks to include in their portfolios.

However, it is important to note that growth investing involves higher risks compared to other investment strategies. The companies targeted by growth investors are often new or relatively small, which means they may be more volatile and susceptible to market fluctuations. Despite these risks, the potential rewards can be substantial. Successful growth investing can lead to dramatic increases in stock prices, offering investors significant capital gains. This risk-reward tradeoff makes growth investing an attractive option for those who are willing to take on higher levels of risk in exchange for the possibility of greater returns.

Understanding industry trends and technological advancements is another crucial aspect of growth investing. Many high-growth companies operate in rapidly evolving industries where staying ahead of trends can make all the difference. For instance, sectors like technology, healthcare, and renewable energy often experience swift changes due to innovation and regulatory shifts. Investors who stay informed about these developments can identify companies that are likely to benefit from emerging trends. Keeping an eye on new technologies, changing consumer preferences, and government policies can help investors select stocks with high growth potential.

6.3 Value Investing

Value investing is a fundamental investment strategy that focuses on identifying undervalued stocks with the potential for significant long-term gains. This approach revolves around the concept of buying low and selling high, but it goes beyond mere price action. Value investors seek to purchase stocks that are trading below their intrinsic value, which is determined through rigorous analysis of various factors such as earnings, assets, and growth potential.

The process of assessing a company's intrinsic value starts with a thorough examination of its financial statements. Earnings, which represent the company's profitability, are a crucial component. Investors look at metrics like earnings per share (EPS) and revenue growth to gauge whether a company is fundamentally strong. Additionally, analyzing a company's assets—both tangible and intangible—helps ascertain if its stock price is justified or undervalued. For instance, a company with valuable patents or a strong brand may have intangible assets that aren't fully reflected in its current stock price.

Growth potential is another important consideration in intrinsic value assessment. A company might show moderate current earnings but has significant growth prospects due to innovations, market expansion, or operational efficiencies. By evaluating these growth opportunities, investors can get a clearer picture of the company's future earnings potential. This comprehensive analysis enables value investors to determine whether a stock is undervalued compared to its true worth.

Finding stocks trading below their intrinsic value is akin to hunting for bargains in the stock market. When a stock trades below its intrinsic value, it means the market has not yet recognized its true potential. This discrepancy can arise from various factors, including market sentiment, economic downturns, or temporary setbacks specific to the company. For example, a company might face short-term challenges such as regulatory issues or supply chain disruptions that depress its stock price. However, if the company's long-term fundamentals remain strong, its stock may be significantly undervalued.

Investing in undervalued stocks allows investors to benefit from future price appreciation as the market eventually corrects its mispricing. Once the broader market recognizes the stock's true value, demand for the stock increases, driving up its price. This price correction can lead to substantial gains for those who invested when the stock was undervalued. The patience and discipline required in value investing often pay off when these undervalued stocks appreciate over time.

One of the core principles of value investing is the importance of a margin of safety. This concept, popularized by Benjamin Graham, emphasizes investing in stocks with a sufficient buffer to protect against potential losses. Essentially, it involves buying stocks at a significant discount to their intrinsic value. This margin of safety acts as a cushion, reducing the risk of losing money even if the investor's valuation turns out to be overly optimistic or external factors negatively impact the company's performance.

The margin of safety is particularly crucial during volatile market conditions. Economic recessions, geopolitical events, or industry-specific downturns can cause stock prices to fluctuate wildly. By investing with a margin of safety, value investors safeguard themselves from steep declines in stock prices. For instance, if a stock is purchased at 30% below its intrinsic value, a market downturn may reduce the stock price by 10%, but the investor still retains a buffer that protects their capital.

A practical example of this principle in action can be seen in Warren Buffett's investment strategies. Known for his value investing prowess, Buffett often seeks companies with strong fundamentals and buys their stocks when they are trading at a discount. His emphasis on a margin of safety has helped him navigate market fluctuations and achieve impressive returns over the long run.

Another distinguishing feature of value investing is taking contrarian positions against prevailing market sentiment. This approach involves buying stocks that are out of favor with most investors. Often, these stocks are neglected or even shunned due to temporary setbacks or negative news. Contrarian value investors see these situations as opportunities to buy quality stocks at discounted prices.

For example, during an economic recession, consumer sentiment might turn overwhelmingly pessimistic, leading to steep declines in stock prices across the board. However, a contrarian value investor might identify solvent companies with robust business models that are simply experiencing a cyclical downturn. By purchasing these stocks when others are selling, the investor can capitalize on the eventual recovery and price appreciation.

This contrarian stance requires a high level of conviction and resilience. Going against the crowd can be psychologically challenging, especially when negative sentiments dominate the headlines. However, history has shown that some of the most lucrative investment opportunities arise when investors dare to swim against the tide. The classic adage "buy when there's blood in the streets" encapsulates this philosophy, suggesting that the best investments are found in times of widespread fear and uncertainty.

6.4 Dividend Investing

Dividend investing offers many advantages for generating regular income and building a diversified portfolio. One of the fundamental principles behind dividend investing is focusing on stocks that pay consistent dividends to create a steady income stream. This approach is particularly appealing to those who seek predictable financial returns without depending solely on market price appreciation. Dividend investors typically look for established companies with strong financial health, ensuring that these businesses can continue paying dividends even during economic downturns.

Investing in dividend-paying stocks requires careful selection and continuous monitoring. Investors often prioritize companies with a history of stable or increasing dividend payments over time. This stability provides a reliable income source that can be reinvested or used for other financial needs. Moreover, dividend-paying stocks are usually less volatile than non-dividend-paying stocks, offering an additional layer of security in an investment portfolio. By incorporating dividend-paying stocks, investors can balance their portfolios, reducing the overall investment risk.

In addition to providing a steady income stream, dividend

investing also has the power to accumulate significant wealth over time through reinvesting dividends. When investors opt to reinvest their dividends, they purchase additional shares of the same company. This reinvestment process not only increases the number of shares owned but also amplifies the potential for future dividend income. Over extended periods, this compounding effect can lead to substantial growth in the value of the investment.

Reinvesting dividends is particularly beneficial in a rising market, where the value of the shares purchased with dividends appreciates along with the original investment. However, the compounding effect works regardless of market conditions, making it a powerful tool for wealth accumulation over the long term. Automated dividend reinvestment plans (DRIPs) offered by many brokerage firms simplify this process and ensure that every dividend payment contributes to growing the investment portfolio.

Dividend-paying stocks often exhibit stability during market downturns, which provides a cushion against volatility. Unlike growth stocks that rely heavily on market sentiment and future earnings potential, dividend-paying stocks are typically associated with more mature companies with established revenue streams. These companies tend to perform relatively well in bear markets because their ability to generate consistent cash flows allows them to maintain dividend payments even during tough economic times.

Moreover, the presence of regular dividend payments can mitigate the impact of falling stock prices. Investors still receive income from dividends, which can be reinvested or used to cover living expenses, even when the market is declining. This feature makes dividend-paying stocks an attractive option for conservative investors who prefer lower-risk investments. The perceived safety and reliability of such stocks can help maintain investor confidence during periods of market turbulence, further stabilizing the stock's price.

Companies that consistently increase dividend payouts signal financial health and growth potential, making them attractive for dividend investors. An increasing dividend payout indicates that a company is confident about its future earnings and cash flow. It shows that the business is capable of generating surplus profits, which can be returned to shareholders. This trend is particularly encouraging for investors seeking both income and capital appreciation since growing dividends often correlate with rising stock prices.

Regularly increasing dividends also reflect positively on a company's management team. It demonstrates a commitment to rewarding shareholders and prudent financial stewardship. Companies with a track record of raising dividends are often seen as having a sustainable competitive advantage, which further enhances their appeal to investors. Such companies become more attractive in the eyes of institutional investors and individual shareholders alike, leading to increased demand for their stocks.

Investors consider several factors when evaluating companies for dividend growth potential. They look at earnings growth, payout ratios, and debt levels to ensure that the company can sustain higher dividend payments. A low payout ratio indicates that the company retains enough earnings to reinvest in its operations while still rewarding its shareholders. Consistently low debt levels suggest financial stability and reduce the likelihood that the company will cut dividends in the future due to financial strain.

6.5 Wrapping It Up

This chapter delved into various investing strategies in the stock market, comparing long-term and short-term approaches, as well as exploring growth, value, and dividend investing. Each of these strategies offers unique benefits and risks that align with different financial goals and risk tolerances.

Reflecting on our discussion of long-term vs. short-term investing, it's clear that the choice between them hinges on your financial objectives and the timeline for achieving them. Long-term investing emphasizes the power of compounding and patience, providing a more stable trajectory through market volatility. It's well-suited for substantial goals like retirement savings or funding education. On the other hand, short-term investing seeks to capitalize on quick market movements, demanding constant vigilance and a high tolerance for risk. While it can offer rapid gains, the associated risks and costs require careful strategy and discipline.

Growth investing appeals to those looking for substantial capital appreciation by targeting companies with robust growth prospects. Identifying such opportunities demands thorough research and a willingness to embrace higher risks for the possibility of greater returns. The focus on emerging trends and innovative sectors can place investors at the forefront of market developments. However, it's essential to remember that growth stocks can be volatile, and their performance can significantly fluctuate based on market conditions.

Value investing stands out with its emphasis on finding under-valued stocks that have the potential for future appreciation. By conducting rigorous analysis to uncover stocks trading below their intrinsic value, investors aim to benefit from eventual market corrections. This approach often involves taking contrarian positions and requires patience for the market to recognize the true worth of these investments. The concept of a margin of safety adds an extra layer of security, making value investing a prudent choice during uncertain times.

Dividend investing offers a more conservative path by focusing on generating steady income from established companies. The predictability of dividends makes this approach appealing for those seeking regular cash flow while also building wealth over time through reinvested dividends. Dividend-paying stocks often exhibit stability, especially during market downturns, providing a buffer against volatility. Companies that consistently increase their dividends signal financial health and growth potential, making them attractive for long-term investors.

As you consider these diverse investment strategies, it's crucial to reflect on your individual financial goals, risk tolerance, and investment horizon. Understanding that each approach has its advantages and challenges will help you make informed decisions that align with your personal circumstances. Market fluctuations are inevitable, and regardless of the strategy you choose, staying disciplined and maintaining a long-term perspective can contribute to your success.

Looking ahead, it's important to remain adaptable and continue learning about market dynamics. The world of investing is always evolving, driven by economic shifts, technological advancements, and changing consumer preferences. By staying informed and open to new opportunities, you can navigate this landscape effectively and work toward achieving your financial goals.

In conclusion, navigating the stock market requires careful consideration of various strategies and an understanding of their implications. Whether you're drawn to the stability of dividends, the potential of growth stocks, the bargain hunting of value investing, or the rapid gains of short-term trading, each path offers valuable lessons and opportunities. As you embark on your investment journey, remember that success comes with ongoing education, patience, and a willingness to adapt. Keep your eyes on the horizon, stay committed to your strategy, and let your financial goals guide you forward.

Chapter 7: Risk Management

Managing and mitigating risks while investing in the stock market is a fundamental skill that can safeguard your financial future. The ups and downs of the market can be as nerve-wracking as they are exhilarating, making it crucial to arm yourself with effective strategies to navigate these fluctuations. Without a well-thought-out approach, even seasoned investors can fall prey to the whims of market volatility. It's about more than just avoiding losses; it's about staying informed, calm, and prepared for whatever the market throws your way. This chapter offers valuable insights into not just riding the waves but mastering them.

In this chapter, we delve into a variety of techniques designed to help you protect your investments amidst uncertain market conditions. You'll learn how to interpret market movements and make decisions based on comprehensive analyses, rather than on fleeting emotions or unfounded hunches. We will discuss the importance of creating a robust investment strategy tailored to your risk tolerance and financial goals. Additionally, we'll explore practical tools like stop-loss orders and hedging to minimize potential losses. By the end of this chapter, you'll have a better understanding of how to make informed decisions that align with long-term investment success, ensuring that you're equipped to handle the inevitable ebb and flow of the stock market.

7.1 Understanding Market Volatility

Understanding market volatility is essential for anyone looking to invest in the stock market. Market ups and downs can be both thrilling and daunting, but being equipped with the right knowledge can help you navigate these changes effectively. Learning how to interpret market movements can significantly impact your decision-making process. For instance, sudden drops may incite panic selling, while quick rises might lead to impulsive buying. It's crucial to remain calm and analytical. Investors should look at a variety of factors such as market trends, company earnings reports, and broader economic indicators before making any decisions. Taking a long-term view and not reacting to every short-term fluctuation can often lead to more stable investment outcomes.

Another key aspect of managing market ups and downs involves creating a solid investment strategy. This includes setting clear financial goals and understanding your own risk tolerance. A diversified portfolio can also help you weather market storms better. By spreading your investments across different asset classes like stocks, bonds, and mutual funds, you reduce the risk of losing everything if one sector takes a hit. Additionally, rebalancing your portfolio periodically ensures that your investment mix remains aligned with your goals and risk appetite. Schwab recommends rebalancing every six or twelve months to keep your risk level consistent with your objectives.

A practical guideline to follow during volatile times is to avoid making hasty decisions based on short-term market movements. Instead, stick to your pre-established investment plan. If you find the market's swings too overwhelming, consider consulting a financial advisor who can provide professional guidance tailored to your situation. This can alleviate some of the emotional stress associated with investing and ensure you're making informed choices.

To gauge market volatility and potential risks, tools like the Cboe Volatility Index (VIX) are invaluable. The VIX measures the market's expectation of 30-day forward-looking volatility and is often referred to as the "fear index." It provides investors with a numeric value representing the market's risk level. A high VIX indicates significant market uncertainty and potential for higher volatility, while a low VIX signals a calmer market. Understanding how to read and interpret the VIX can give you insights into current market conditions and help you adjust your investment strategy accordingly.

Apart from the VIX, other tools can also help gauge market volatility. For example, moving averages and Bollinger Bands offer visual representations of price action and volatility over specific periods. Technical analysis tools, including Relative Strength Index (RSI) and Average True Range (ATR), further enable you to assess market momentum and volatility. These tools can help you identify potential entry and exit points in your investments, reducing the risk of making poorly-timed decisions. Utilizing multiple tools ensures a more comprehensive understanding of market dynamics.

It's important to treat these tools as part of a broader strategy. Relying solely on technical indicators without considering fundamental factors can be risky. Always complement your technical analysis with a review of economic data, company performance reports, and other relevant information. This holistic approach ensures that your investment decisions are well-rounded and based on a variety of reliable inputs.

Studying past market behaviors is another effective way to prepare for potential future volatility. Historical data provides valuable lessons on how markets have reacted to different events and conditions. For example, analyzing market responses to past financial crises, technological advancements, or significant policy changes can offer insights into how similar future events might impact the market. Reviewing this data helps you identify patterns and trends that could be indicative of upcoming volatility.

Understanding historical trends requires access to comprehensive financial databases and analytical tools. Many financial institutions offer resources and platforms that allow investors to simulate different market scenarios using historical data. These simulations can help you develop strategies for various market conditions, ensuring you're better prepared for whatever the market throws at you. Additionally, reviewing expert analyses and commentaries on past market events can provide context and deepen your understanding.

It's also beneficial to learn from seasoned investors who have successfully navigated market volatility over the years. Reading books, attending webinars, and following reputable financial advisors can provide practical tips and strategies grounded in real-world experience. This knowledge can be applied to your own investing practices, helping you avoid common pitfalls and make informed decisions during turbulent times.

Analyzing factors that cause market fluctuations is crucial for anticipating and mitigating risks. Economic indicators such as gross domestic product (GDP) growth rates, unemployment rates, and inflation levels play a significant role in market movements. Positive economic data generally boosts investor confidence, leading to bullish markets, while negative data can trigger sell-offs and increased volatility. Staying informed about these indicators enables you to understand the underlying forces driving market changes.

Geopolitical events are another major driver of market fluctuations. Political instability, trade disputes, and conflicts can create uncertainty and affect global markets. For instance, Brexit negotiations had a profound impact on both European and global financial markets. Similarly, tensions between major economies like the U.S. and China can lead to market volatility. Keeping abreast of geopolitical developments allows you to anticipate potential market disruptions and adjust your investment strategy accordingly.

Corporate earnings reports and business cycles are additional factors influencing market behavior. Companies regularly release quarterly earnings reports that detail their financial performance. Strong earnings can boost stock prices, while disappointing results can lead to declines. Understanding how to interpret these reports and recognizing cyclical patterns in various industries can help you predict market movements and make timely investment decisions.

7.2 Setting Stop-Loss Orders

Stop-loss orders are an essential tool in risk management for investors. At their core, a stop-loss order is a directive given to a broker to buy or sell a stock once it reaches a specific price. This mechanism helps investors protect themselves from significant losses by pre-determining the maximum loss they are willing to accept on a particular investment. By setting these orders, investors can ensure that their stocks will be sold automatically if prices drop to a certain level, thereby limiting potential losses.

The significance of stop-loss orders lies in their ability to offer peace of mind and reduce emotional decision-making. When investing in the stock market, it's easy to become swayed by emotions such as fear and greed. These emotions can lead to impulsive decisions that might not align with one's long-term investment strategy. By using stop-loss orders, investors can detach their emotions from the trading process, relying on predetermined rules to guide their actions instead. This structured approach can contribute to more consistent and disciplined investing practices.

Moreover, understanding how to properly implement stop-loss orders can contribute to overall portfolio stability. They provide a straightforward way of managing downside risks without the need for constant monitoring of market movements. For working professionals and college students who may not have the time or expertise to keep track of their investments daily, stop-loss orders serve as a valuable tool for keeping their portfolios aligned with their risk tolerance and financial goals.

Setting effective stop-loss levels is crucial for maximizing the benefits of this risk management tool. One method for determining the optimal level is to consider one's risk tolerance, which varies from investor to investor. Risk tolerance is influenced by factors such as financial goals, investment horizon, and overall financial situation. Investors should honestly evaluate how much loss they can endure on any given trade before setting their stop-loss levels.

Another strategy involves analyzing historical price data and volatility of the particular stock in question. Understanding a stock's typical price fluctuations can help in setting more informed stop-loss levels. For instance, setting a stop-loss too close to the current market price might result in premature selling due to regular market noise. Conversely, setting it too far could expose the investor to more significant losses than they are comfortable with. A balance needs to be struck, considering both personal risk tolerance and the stock's behavior.

It's also beneficial to regularly review and adjust stop-loss orders as per the evolving market conditions. Markets are dynamic, and so is the performance of individual stocks. As new information becomes available or as significant changes occur in the business environment affecting the stock, adjustments to stop-loss levels might be necessary. This ongoing evaluation ensures that the set levels remain relevant and continue to protect the investor's capital effectively.

Monitoring and adjusting stop-loss orders is another critical aspect of effective risk management. While initial settings are vital, the ability to adapt to market changes is equally important. Investors should periodically reassess their stop-loss orders to ensure they still align with their investment strategies and current market conditions. Regularly checking these orders can help avoid unnecessary trade executions triggered by temporary market volatility.

There are several techniques for monitoring and adjusting stop-loss orders. One approach is to use trailing stop-loss orders. Unlike fixed stop-losses, trailing stops move with the price of the stock. If the stock price rises, the trailing stop adjusts upward, helping lock in gains while still offering protection if the price falls. This technique provides a dynamic safety net that adapts to favorable market conditions without requiring continuous manual adjustments.

Investors should also stay informed about major market events or news that could impact the stocks they hold. Significant corporate announcements, economic reports, or geopolitical developments can cause abrupt price movements. By staying updated, investors can swiftly adjust their stop-loss orders to reflect any newfound risk or opportunity, ensuring their investments are adequately protected irrespective of market conditions.

Examining the advantages and drawbacks of stop-loss orders helps investors decide whether this tool fits their overall strategy. One primary advantage is the ability to limit losses without requiring constant market monitoring. This feature makes stop-loss orders particularly useful for those unable to dedicate substantial time to tracking their investments. Additionally, by automating the sale of a stock at a predetermined price, stop-loss orders remove emotional bias from trading decisions and foster a more disciplined approach.

However, there are drawbacks to consider. For instance, in highly volatile markets, stop-loss orders might trigger prematurely due to short-term price swings, resulting in the sale of stocks that might otherwise have recovered. This scenario could lead to missed opportunities and potentially lower returns. Moreover, stop-loss orders don't guarantee execution at the exact stop price, especially during periods of high market volatility or low liquidity, where the actual sale price could be significantly different from the set stop price.

Understanding the appropriate contexts for using stop-loss orders is key. In stable or steadily rising markets, stop-loss orders can effectively safeguard against sudden downturns. Conversely, in turbulent markets, where prices frequently oscillate, a more cautious approach might be warranted to prevent unwanted triggers. Balancing the frequency and distance of stop-loss orders based on careful market analysis helps mitigate some of the inherent risks while leveraging their protective benefits.

7.3 Hedging Your Investments

Hedging is a fundamental strategy in risk management designed to protect investment portfolios from adverse market movements. The primary purpose of hedging is to reduce potential losses and provide stability to an investor's portfolio. Understanding the various methods used for hedging against market risks is crucial for any investor looking to safeguard their financial assets. Hedging involves taking offsetting positions in related securities, which can limit losses if the primary investment moves unfavorably.

One common method of hedging involves derivatives, such as options. Options give investors the right, but not the obligation, to buy or sell an asset at a predetermined price. For instance, purchasing put options allows an investor to sell a stock at a specific price, providing protection if the stock's price declines. Another method includes futures contracts, which obligate the buyer to purchase and the seller to sell a specific asset at a future date and price. By locking in prices, futures can shield investors from price volatility.

In addition to derivatives and futures, put options are also widely used in hedging strategies. A put option increases in value as the underlying asset decreases, thus offering downside protection. These instruments are particularly beneficial in volatile markets where sudden drops are likely. By employing these methods, investors can create a financial buffer against unexpected downturns, ensuring more predictable outcomes.

Beyond understanding these methods, it is important to explore the various types of hedging instruments available to investors. Derivatives are versatile tools that can be customized to fit specific hedging needs. They include options, forwards, swaps, and futures. Each derivative has unique characteristics that cater to different risk management objectives. For example, swaps can help manage interest rate risks, while forwards can lock in exchange rates for currency risk management.

Futures contracts, another type of derivative, provide leverage, allowing investors to control large positions with relatively small capital outlays. This leverage can amplify gains but also magnify losses, making it essential for investors to use them judiciously. Futures are commonly used by institutional investors for commodity hedging but can also be applied to financial assets like stocks and bonds.

Put options, specifically, stand out due to their ability to offer direct protection against declines in asset prices. When concerns over market corrections arise, buying put options on indexes like the S&P 500 can hedge against broad market declines. This approach is particularly useful when investors anticipate overall market volatility rather than individual stock fluctuations.

Implementing hedge strategies effectively requires practical knowledge of how to apply these techniques in varying market scenarios. When markets are bullish, investors might use protective puts to guard against potential corrections without missing out on further gains. In contrast, during bearish markets, strategies like covered calls may be more appropriate, where investors sell call options on assets they own, generating income while preparing for further declines.

Diversification is another practical approach in hedging. By spreading investments across different asset classes, sectors, and geographical regions, investors can mitigate risks associated with any single market segment. This not only reduces exposure to market-specific events but also smoothens overall portfolio performance.

Moreover, dynamic hedging, which involves continuously adjusting hedges based on market conditions, ensures that the protection remains effective. This might involve rebalancing the portfolio periodically or modifying existing hedges to align with changing market dynamics. Such proactive measures are essential in maintaining the effectiveness of hedging strategies throughout different market cycles.

Evaluating the costs and benefits of different hedging instruments and strategies is critical to making informed decisions. The cost of hedging can sometimes outweigh the benefits, especially in stable market conditions. For instance, buying options require paying premiums, which can erode returns if the anticipated market movement does not occur. Therefore, investors must weigh the potential loss savings against these costs.

An effective hedge should appreciate in value as the underlying asset depreciates, offsetting any losses. However, it's equally important to consider liquidity, ease of implementation, and tax implications when selecting hedging instruments. Some instruments may have favorable tax treatments, potentially easing the financial burden associated with hedging activities.

Furthermore, investors need to assess their risk tolerance and investment horizon. Short-term hedges may be suitable for those expecting immediate market volatility, while long-term investors might prefer strategies that provide ongoing protection. Balancing these factors helps tailor hedging strategies to meet specific investment goals.

7.4 Managing Emotional Reactions to Market Fluctuations

Understanding common biases that influence investment decisions is crucial for developing emotional resilience and discipline. One prevalent bias is the "overconfidence bias," where investors overestimate their knowledge or predictive abilities regarding market movements. This overconfidence can lead to excessive trading, taking on high risk, and ultimately substantial losses. Recognizing this bias helps investors stay grounded and make more informed decisions based on thorough research rather than gut feelings or unfounded beliefs about their market prowess.

Another common bias is "loss aversion," which refers to the tendency to fear losses more than valuing gains of an equivalent amount. This psychological effect often results in holding onto losing stocks for too long, hoping they will rebound, while quickly selling winners to lock in profits. Understanding loss aversion can aid investors in making more balanced decisions. Instead of reacting emotionally to potential losses, one should focus on the bigger picture and long-term strategy, ensuring that each decision aligns with overall financial goals.

Additionally, there's the "herd mentality," where individuals follow the majority in investment decisions, assuming that the crowd's actions must be correct. This behavior can drive market bubbles and crashes when many investors enter or exit positions simultaneously. By being aware of this bias, investors can strive to conduct independent analyses and base their choices on personal research and risk tolerance rather than blindly following market trends or the latest hype.

In times of market turbulence, maintaining objectivity and staying rational becomes paramount. One effective strategy is to develop a solid investment plan before entering the market, outlining specific goals, risk tolerance levels, and time horizons. When market conditions get rough, having this plan as a reference can provide clarity and prevent impulsive decisions driven by short-term market movements.

Another approach is to diversify investments across various asset classes. Diversification reduces the impact of any single investment's poor performance on the overall portfolio, providing a buffer against volatility. For example, combining stocks, bonds, and other asset types can help mitigate risks and maintain steadier returns even during market downturns. This strategy encourages a broader perspective and minimizes the temptation to react emotionally to individual stock price changes.

Moreover, practicing mindfulness and stress management techniques such as deep breathing, meditation, or regular physical exercise can keep emotions in check. Staying calm and composed allows investors to think clearly and logically, making well-considered decisions. It's essential to recognize that market volatility is inevitable and temporary. Remaining focused on long-term goals rather than short-term fluctuations helps in maintaining a level-headed approach during turbulent times.

Establishing personal guidelines is another key aspect of preventing emotional responses from impacting investment choices. Setting rules for buying, holding, and selling investments can create a disciplined approach resistant to emotional whims. For example, defining a maximum percentage of portfolio allocation to any single stock can prevent overexposure to one company or sector, limiting potential losses.

Having predetermined criteria for exiting investments is also crucial. This could involve setting stop-loss orders, which automatically sell a stock when it falls to a certain price, or establishing profit targets that trigger a sale when a stock reaches a particular gain. These guidelines provide a structured approach to selling, removing emotional bias from the process and helping investors avoid panic selling during market dips or getting overly greedy during rallies.

Regularly reviewing and updating these guidelines ensures they remain relevant and aligned with evolving financial goals and market conditions. Sticking to established rules requires discipline but provides stability and predictability in decision-making. Over time, this consistent approach fosters confidence and reduces anxiety related to market fluctuations.

Techniques for self-assessment and mental conditioning are valuable tools for improving emotional control in investing. Regularly evaluating one's emotional state and identifying triggers that lead to impulsive decisions can help in developing strategies to manage these reactions. Journaling investment decisions and reflecting on the reasoning behind them can provide insights into patterns of behavior and areas needing improvement.

Mental conditioning involves training oneself to respond to market events with measured actions rather than knee-jerk reactions. Visualization techniques, where one imagines various market scenarios and plans appropriate responses, can prepare the mind to handle actual situations calmly. Additionally, studying successful investors' approaches and philosophies can offer perspectives and strategies to emulate.

Building a support network of fellow investors or a mentor can also contribute to better emotional control. Sharing experiences, discussing strategies, and receiving feedback can help validate one's approach and provide reassurance during uncertain times. This sense of community can reduce feelings of isolation and bolster confidence in sticking to well-thought-out plans despite market noise.

7.5 Wrapping It Up

In this chapter, we've explored essential techniques to manage and mitigate risks while investing in the stock market. Understanding market volatility is crucial for making informed decisions and safeguarding your investments. By staying calm and analytical, you can better interpret market trends and make more stable investment choices.

We discussed how creating a solid investment strategy involves setting clear financial goals, understanding your risk tolerance, and diversifying your portfolio. These steps help you weather market storms more effectively and ensure that your investments stay aligned with your objectives. Rebalancing your portfolio periodically ensures that it remains consistent with your risk level and goals.

During volatile times, it's important to avoid making hasty decisions based on short-term market movements. Instead, stick to your pre-established investment plan and consider seeking advice from a financial advisor if needed. Professional guidance can alleviate some of the stress associated with investing and help you make more informed choices.

Using tools like the Cboe Volatility Index (VIX) and other technical analysis tools can provide valuable insights into current market conditions. These tools help you gauge market risk levels and adjust your investment strategy accordingly. However, remember to complement technical analysis with fundamental factors such as economic data and company performance reports for a well-rounded approach.

Studying past market behaviors and learning from seasoned investors can also prepare you for potential future volatility. Analyzing historical data and recognizing patterns can offer insights into how similar events might impact the market. This knowledge allows you to develop strategies for various market conditions.

Setting stop-loss orders is another vital risk management tool.

Stop-loss orders help protect your investments by ensuring that your stocks are sold automatically if prices drop to a specific level. This mechanism offers peace of mind and reduces emotional decision-making, contributing to a more disciplined investing practice.

Hedging your investments provides additional protection against adverse market movements. By using derivatives, futures, and options, you can create a financial buffer that limits potential losses. Implementing these strategies requires a thorough understanding of different hedging instruments and their applications in varying market scenarios.

Managing emotional reactions to market fluctuations is equally important. Recognizing common biases like overconfidence, loss aversion, and herd mentality can help you make more balanced decisions. Developing a solid investment plan, diversifying your assets, and practicing mindfulness techniques can keep your emotions in check during turbulent times.

By following these strategies and remaining disciplined, you can navigate the ups and downs of the stock market more effectively. The key is to stay informed, stick to your plan, and continuously evaluate and adjust your investments based on changing market conditions.

As you move forward, keep these principles in mind and continue building on the knowledge you've gained. Investing in the stock market involves constant learning and adaptation. Take what you've learned here and be prepared for whatever the market throws at you. Always stay proactive, informed, and resilient—these qualities will serve you well in your investment journey.

Chapter 8: Staying Informed and Continuously Learning

Staying informed and continuously learning are essential practices for anyone looking to succeed in the stock market. The ever-changing landscape of financial markets demands that investors stay updated with the latest news, trends, and developments. By keeping abreast of current market conditions and educating themselves on intricate investment strategies, both novice and seasoned investors can make well-informed decisions. In this chapter, we delve into these foundational aspects of investing, shedding light on how to remain knowledgeable and adaptable in a dynamic environment.

We'll start by exploring the importance of following reliable financial news sources to gather accurate information about market movements. Next, we discuss the value of subscribing to newsletters and alerts, which provide timely updates that help investors react promptly to changes. Additionally, we'll cover the critical need to vet news sources to avoid misinformation. Beyond just staying informed, we'll also highlight various educational resources such as online courses, webinars, and financial literature that deepen your understanding of the market. The chapter emphasizes interpreting key metrics and trends from market reports and the benefits of joining investment communities. By the end, you'll have a robust toolkit for continuous learning and informed decision-making in your investment journey.

8.1 Following Financial News and Reports

Staying informed is crucial for investors who want to make sound decisions in the stock market. One of the best ways to ensure you are well-informed is by utilizing reputable financial news sources. These sources provide accurate and timely information about market trends, economic developments, and company performance. By consistently following trusted news outlets, investors can gain insights that may influence their investment choices.

Reliable financial news sources like Bloomberg, The Wall Street Journal, and CNBC offer comprehensive coverage of various market segments and financial events. These platforms employ experienced journalists and financial analysts who interpret complex data and trends, making it easier for investors to understand the market's direction. Relying on such credible sources helps investors avoid the pitfalls of misinformation and stay ahead of the curve in a fast-paced market environment.

Moreover, subscribing to newsletters or alerts from these reputable sources ensures that investors receive the latest updates directly in their inboxes. This proactive approach enables them to act swiftly on new information, whether it's a significant earnings report, economic data release, or geopolitical event affecting the markets. Staying updated through trustworthy channels can significantly impact the effectiveness of one's investment strategy.

Being selective about news sources is equally important because not all information available online or offline is reliable. There is a plethora of financial news, and often, some sources may publish unverified, biased, or incomplete information. Investors need to critically evaluate their news sources to avoid being swayed by inaccurate reports that could lead to poor investment decisions.

One way to vet news sources is by checking their track record and reputation within the investment community. Look for sources with a history of accurate reporting and see if they are frequently cited by other respected publications. Websites with clear editorial standards and transparent fact-checking processes are generally more credible. Additionally, cross-referencing news across multiple trusted platforms can help verify the accuracy of the information.

It's also essential to be cautious of sensational headlines designed to attract clicks rather than inform. These articles often exaggerate or misrepresent facts, leading to misguided perceptions about market conditions. By prioritizing news sources known for their integrity and depth of analysis, investors can filter out noise and focus on the most relevant and accurate market information.

Regularly checking news updates is vital for investors to react promptly to market changes. The stock market is dynamic, and prices can fluctuate rapidly in response to new information.

By staying abreast of the latest developments, investors can seize opportunities or mitigate risks before others do. Regular updates help investors remain agile and responsive to market movements.

Setting aside specific times during the day to review news updates can create a disciplined routine. For instance, checking news at the beginning and end of each trading day can help investors prepare for potential market moves and assess the day's performance. Many financial news websites and apps offer customizable alerts for critical updates, ensuring that investors receive instant notifications about major events.

Additionally, during times of heightened market volatility, keeping a closer eye on news updates becomes even more crucial. Economic indicators, corporate earnings releases, and significant policy announcements can dramatically affect market sentiment. By staying informed through regular checks, investors can adjust their portfolios as needed, aligning them with the current market environment.

Interpreting key metrics and trends in market reports is an essential skill for making informed investment decisions. Financial news often includes data and statistics that reflect market health and individual company performance. Understanding these metrics can guide investors in evaluating investment opportunities and potential risks.

Market reports usually contain information like earnings per share (EPS), price-to-earnings (P/E) ratios, revenue growth, and debt levels. Knowing how to read and interpret these figures

allows investors to compare companies within the same industry and identify those with strong fundamentals. For example,
a company with consistent revenue growth and manageable
debt may be a more attractive investment compared to one with
unpredictable earnings and high leverage.

Additionally, broader market trends such as changes in interest
rates, inflation, and unemployment rates can provide context
for individual stock performance. Investors who understand
these macroeconomic indicators can better anticipate how
different sectors might be affected. For instance, rising interest
rates typically negatively impact high-growth tech stocks but
may benefit financial institutions.

Analyzing historical trends within market reports can also
uncover patterns that repeat over time. Observing how certain
stocks or sectors performed under similar economic conditions
in the past can provide insights into future performance. This
historical perspective, combined with current data interpreta-
tion, equips investors with a comprehensive view necessary for
strategic decision-making.

8.2 Using Educational Resources and Tools

Utilizing educational resources and tools is crucial for enhancing one's understanding of the stock market. Participating
in online courses and webinars can significantly deepen your
knowledge about stock market concepts. These resources are
designed to offer structured learning pathways that start with
basic principles and advance to more complex topics. Many
platforms provide interactive features such as quizzes, live

sessions, and discussion forums, allowing learners to engage actively with the material and instructors.

Online courses often cover a wide range of subjects, from fundamental analyses, technical analyses, risk management, to behavioral finance. Taking these courses enables you to understand not just the 'how' but also the 'why' behind market movements. Webinars, on the other hand, tend to be more focused on specific current issues or trends in the market. They often feature live Q&A sessions where participants can ask questions and get immediate answers from experts, making them highly valuable for real-time learning and application.

Moreover, the convenience of online courses and webinars cannot be overstated. Participants can learn at their own pace and on their schedule, making it easier to balance learning with other professional or personal responsibilities. This flexibility makes these educational tools accessible to working professionals and students alike, providing everyone the opportunity to improve their investing skills without disrupting their daily routines.

Accessing expert-led educational content can clarify complex investment topics. Many investors find certain aspects of the stock market intricate and challenging to master. Expert-led content simplifies this complexity by breaking down advanced topics into understandable segments. For instance, financial modeling, options trading, and algorithmic trading are areas that require specialized knowledge. Experts put these complex subjects into perspective, offering simplified explanations, practical examples, and case studies.

Expert-led content also provides insights that might not be readily available through traditional learning methods. Seasoned investors share their real-world experiences, tips, and strategies, which can be invaluable for new investors. By learning from those who have already navigated the complexities of the market, aspiring investors can avoid common pitfalls and adopt best practices more quickly.

In addition, much expert-led content includes up-to-date analyses of current market conditions. This ensures that learners are not only gaining theoretical knowledge but also understanding how to apply it in the present-day market. This dual focus on theory and application enhances an investor's ability to make informed decisions based on both historical data and current trends.

Reading financial literature and research papers can provide valuable insights into market trends. Financial literature encompasses a broad spectrum of writings including books, journals, articles, and whitepapers. This literary wealth offers diverse perspectives and deep dives into various facets of the stock market. Authors often explore overarching themes like economic indicators, market cycles, and investor psychology, which provide readers with a comprehensive understanding of how different factors interconnect to influence market behavior.

Research papers, often backed by data and conducted by scholars or industry specialists, add another layer of depth to one's understanding. These papers analyze market trends, testing hypotheses and presenting findings that challenge conventional wisdom. For example, academic studies on market anomalies or the efficacy of technical analysis tools provide empirical evidence on what works and what doesn't, helping investors refine their strategies.

Another advantage of reading financial literature is exposure to different analytical frameworks and methodologies. Investors can learn about valuation models, quantitative approaches, and qualitative assessments that may be outside their current knowledge base. This broader understanding equips them to evaluate investment opportunities from multiple angles, enhancing their decision-making prowess.

Studying renowned investment literature can offer diverse perspectives on investing strategies. Legendary investors like Warren Buffett, Peter Lynch, and Benjamin Graham have authored books that have become seminal works in the field of investment. Reading these classics allows investors to understand the fundamental principles that guided some of the most successful investors of our time. These works delve into timeless strategies, such as value investing, growth investing, and contrarian investing, providing a well-rounded education on different approaches to the market.

Each of these investment philosophies offers unique insights into managing risks and identifying opportunities. For instance, Benjamin Graham's "The Intelligent Investor" emphasizes the importance of thorough analysis and a long-term outlook, while Peter Lynch's "One Up On Wall Street" encourages finding undervalued stocks through diligent research. By absorbing these varying viewpoints, investors can develop a more nuanced approach that incorporates elements from multiple strategies to suit their individual goals and risk tolerance.

Additionally, investment literature often includes autobiographical elements that offer glimpses into the thought processes and life experiences that shaped these iconic figures' investment philosophies. Understanding the mindset of successful investors can inspire and guide new investors in developing their mental models for navigating the complexities of the stock market.

8.3 Joining Investment Communities

Joining investment communities offers numerous advantages for budding and seasoned investors alike. One significant benefit is the opportunity to participate in online forums and social media groups where individuals can discuss investment strategies. These platforms are abundant with resources, ranging from articles and tutorials to interactive discussions that provide investors with valuable insights into various investment techniques. By joining these forums, investors can stay updated on the latest market trends and acquire knowledge from a diverse group of voices. Being part of such communities ensures that members are always learning and adapting to new information, ultimately refining their investment approaches over time.

In addition to the wealth of information available, online forums foster an environment of continuous learning. Members frequently share their experiences, ask questions, and engage in debates about best practices and emerging trends. This collaborative culture helps individuals to identify potential pitfalls and opportunities they might not have considered on their own. For example, a forum discussion might highlight a particular stock's hidden risk or unveil a promising investment avenue, thereby equipping participants with a broader understanding of the market.

Moreover, social media groups often feature real-time updates and alerts concerning market developments. These timely notifications can be crucial for making informed investment decisions. For instance, when a significant market event occurs, members of these groups can quickly share their analyses and predictions, helping others react promptly and wisely. Engaging in these conversations not only keeps investors informed but also allows them to witness how more experienced members interpret and respond to market changes.

While it's beneficial to discuss investment strategies, engaging with diverse opinions within these communities can significantly broaden one's perspective on market trends. Exposure to varying viewpoints enables investors to develop a well-rounded understanding of the market landscape. This variety of perspectives is essential because it challenges preconceived notions and encourages critical thinking. When investors consider alternative opinions, they are better positioned to anticipate potential market shifts and adapt their strategies accordingly.

For example, an investor might initially be highly optimistic about a particular sector but could encounter cautionary advice from other community members who have observed underlying risks. Such interactions cultivate a more balanced approach to investing, reducing the likelihood of falling victim to hype or unfounded optimism. By critically evaluating different viewpoints, investors learn to weigh the pros and cons of each situation more effectively, leading to more rational and less emotional decision-making.

Furthermore, engaging with diverse opinions can help investors identify emerging trends before they become mainstream. Community members often share insights based on their unique experiences or specialized knowledge, which can unveil new opportunities. For instance, a member who closely follows tech startups might notice a trend in AI development that others have overlooked. Such early detection of trends can position investors ahead of the curve, providing a competitive edge in the market.

Networking with experienced investors is another invaluable advantage of joining investment communities. These seasoned professionals bring a wealth of knowledge and practical expertise that can guide less experienced members. Through networking, novices can gain mentorship, receive personalized advice, and learn about the intricacies of investment strategies that are not typically covered in standard educational materials. A mentor can offer guidance on navigating tricky market conditions, identifying high-potential investments, and avoiding common mistakes.

Mentorship within investment communities fosters a supportive environment where experienced investors willingly share their wisdom and success stories. These interactions allow newcomers to benefit from the hard-earned lessons of their mentors, accelerating their learning curve. An experienced mentor might, for example, teach a mentee how to analyze financial statements more effectively or show them how to use certain analytical tools to predict stock performance better.

Additionally, networking with experienced investors provides access to exclusive investment opportunities that might otherwise be unavailable to individual investors. Seasoned professionals often have established connections within the industry and can introduce their protégés to private deals, upcoming IPOs, or niche markets. These introductions can significantly enhance an investor's portfolio and open doors to investments that promise high returns but require insider knowledge or connections to access.

Local investment clubs also play a critical role in fostering an environment conducive to practical learning. These clubs offer face-to-face interactions that can complement the virtual exchanges happening in online communities. By joining local investment clubs, members can meet regularly to discuss market strategies, share insights, and collectively evaluate investment opportunities. The hands-on experience gained through participation in these clubs is invaluable for understanding the nuances of investing.

One of the main benefits of local investment clubs is the opportunity for collaborative investment activities. These clubs often pool resources to invest in larger projects or portfolios, allowing members to diversify their investments without bearing all the risks individually. This collective approach enables participants to learn about various asset classes and investment vehicles, from real estate and stocks to mutual funds and bonds. Through these collaborations, members gain practical experience and sharpen their investment skills.

Moreover, sharing experiences within local clubs creates a supportive learning environment where members feel encouraged to ask questions, seek advice, and share their successes and failures. This culture of openness and collaboration helps build confidence, especially among novice investors who might feel intimidated by the complexity of the financial markets. As members share their journeys, others can learn from their experiences and avoid similar pitfalls, fostering a community of continuous improvement.

8.4 Learning from Your Investment Experiences

Reflecting on past investment experiences holds immense significance for investors aiming to refine and improve their future decisions. By monitoring the performance of past investments, you can gain valuable insights into your decision-making processes. This involves analyzing both the qualitative and quantitative aspects of each investment to identify what worked well and what didn't. Keeping a close eye on how different stocks or other assets performed over time allows you to discern patterns and trends that could be influencing your portfolio's success or failure. For instance, if a particular sector consistently underperforms in your portfolio, it might prompt you to reassess your allocation strategy for that sector.

One practical method for tracking investment performance

is to use a spreadsheet or dedicated software where you can log each investment's entry and exit points along with any dividends received. Regularly updating this data will help you keep track of how much profit or loss each investment generates, providing clear evidence of your investment prowess. This approach also helps you stay objective by relying on hard data rather than gut feelings or anecdotal experiences. Furthermore, monitoring performance isn't solely about individual stocks; it should include an overview of your entire portfolio's health to ensure diversification goals are met, risk is managed, and overall growth remains in line with your financial objectives.

Incorporating feedback loops into your investment process can also be beneficial. By routinely reviewing the outcomes of your investments, you develop a habit of continuous learning and improvement. This reflective practice not only enhances your understanding of the market but also fosters a disciplined approach to investing. For example, after a significant market event, analyzing how your investments reacted can provide insights into whether your current strategies are robust or need adjustment. Reflecting on past experiences encourages a proactive mindset, allowing you to make informed changes before small issues evolve into significant problems.

Analyzing gains and losses is another crucial aspect of refining investment strategies. Delving into why certain investments yielded positive returns while others did not can illuminate key factors that contribute to successful investing. For instance, was a profitable stock tied to sound fundamentals like robust earnings reports and market share growth? Conversely, understanding why some investments resulted in losses can be equally enlightening. Did those losses stem from external factors such as economic downturns, or were they due to mis-judgments like overestimating a company's growth potential?

By conducting post-mortem analyses of your investments, you can pinpoint recurring mistakes and avoid them in the future. Perhaps you notice a tendency to hold onto losing stocks for too long, hoping for a turnaround that's unlikely to happen. Acknowledging this pattern can lead to setting stricter sell criteria or stop-loss orders to mitigate future losses. On the flip side, recognizing strategies that consistently result in gains allows you to double down on these methods, improving your overall portfolio performance.

Additionally, comparing your investment outcomes with broader market performance can provide context for your results. If your portfolio underperformed the market, identifying the underlying reasons—whether it's sector-specific downturns or poor stock picks—can guide better decision-making. Analyzing gains and losses equips you with a deeper understanding of market dynamics and personal biases, fostering more effective investment strategies moving forward.

Documenting investment outcomes serves as a practical guide for making informed adjustments in your future plans. Main-taining a detailed record of each investment, including the rationale behind initial decisions, subsequent actions taken, and final results, creates a valuable resource to consult over time. This documentation helps you build a history of your investment journey, making it easier to recall the thought process and circumstances surrounding specific decisions.

Having a comprehensive investment journal ensures that lessons learned from previous investments are preserved and utilized. For instance, if a particular investment performed poorly due to insufficient research, documenting this experience encourages thorough analysis for future opportunities. Similarly, noting the success factors of profitable investments provides a blueprint for replicating such outcomes. This habit fosters a culture of accountability and continuous improvement, essential traits for successful long-term investing.

Moreover, written records help you maintain consistency in applying your investment strategy. They serve as reference points to check whether you're adhering to your predetermined criteria for buying, holding, and selling securities. By regularly reviewing documented outcomes, you can ensure your investment decisions align with your overarching financial goals and risk tolerance. This systematic approach minimizes impulsive decisions based on short-term market fluctuations, promoting a more disciplined investment practice.

Adapting investment approaches based on past experiences is crucial for mitigating future risks. The stock market is dynamic, and strategies that worked in the past may not always be effective in changing conditions. By reflecting on previous investments, you can identify which methods need tweaking to better suit current market environments. This adaptability ensures your investment approach remains relevant and resilient against unforeseen challenges.

For example, a value investing strategy that thrived during

a bear market might need adjustment in a booming economy where growth stocks outperform. Learning from past experiences enables you to pivot your strategy accordingly, perhaps incorporating elements of growth investing to capture higher returns during bullish periods. Flexibility in modifying your investment approach based on historical insights can safeguard your portfolio from stagnation and enhance its growth potential.

Furthermore, adapting based on past experiences fosters a proactive risk management mindset. Recognizing patterns of market volatility and adjusting your strategy to buffer against such risks can prevent significant losses. For instance, if past investments suffered during economic downturns due to high exposure to volatile sectors, reallocating assets to more stable investments like bonds or blue-chip stocks can provide a safety net. This continual adaptation strengthens your portfolio's resilience, ensuring sustained performance irrespective of market fluctuations.

8.5 Wrapping It Up

Throughout this chapter, we've explored the crucial role of continuous education and staying updated on market trends in making informed investment decisions. By following reliable financial news sources, utilizing educational resources and tools, joining investment communities, and learning from your experiences, you equip yourself with the knowledge needed to navigate the dynamic nature of the stock market.

Consistently gaining insights from reputable financial news

platforms like Bloomberg, The Wall Street Journal, and CNBC, helps you stay ahead in a fast-paced environment. These sources provide valuable information that can influence your investment choices and keep you informed about market developments. Remember, being selective with your sources is vital to avoid misinformation and ensure you base your decisions on accurate data.

Educational resources such as online courses and webinars offer structured learning pathways for deepening your understanding of stock market concepts. Expert-led content simplifies complex topics, while financial literature allows you to explore diverse perspectives and analytical frameworks. Engaging in these resources helps you grasp both the theoretical and practical aspects of investing, enhancing your ability to make sound decisions.

Joining investment communities, whether online forums or local clubs, provides a platform for continuous learning through shared experiences and diverse opinions. Networking with experienced investors offers invaluable mentorship and access to exclusive opportunities, fostering a supportive environment where you can grow and refine your strategies. Such interactions broaden your perspective, helping you anticipate market shifts and adapt accordingly.

Reflecting on past investment experiences is another key element in improving your decision-making process. By monitoring the performance of your investments, analyzing gains and losses, and documenting outcomes, you build a history that guides future adjustments. This continuous learning loop ensures that you remain flexible and resilient in the face of changing market conditions.

Being proactive in your approach to investing involves a commitment to staying educated and informed. The stock market is inherently dynamic, meaning past strategies may not always be effective, but by learning and adapting, you can better prepare for future challenges. This mindset of ongoing education and reflection enables you to make informed decisions and turn potential pitfalls into opportunities.

Ultimately, your journey in the stock market is one of constant evolution. As you continue to gather knowledge and experience, you'll become more adept at navigating its complexities. Staying curious, open-minded, and committed to learning will serve you well, no matter how the market evolves. So, keep exploring, questioning, and adapting—your future self will thank you for it.

Conclusion

As you come to the end of this book, take a moment to reflect on your journey. When you first opened these pages, you might have felt overwhelmed by terms like "diversification," "portfolio," and "market trends." Now, consider how far you've come. Think back to that initial feeling of uncertainty and compare it to the knowledge and confidence you hold today. You've grown immensely in understanding the stock market and investing principles.

When you first started reading, you likely had many questions about where and how to begin investing. The stock market can indeed seem like a daunting place, full of complexities and jargon that can easily intimidate even the most determined beginner. But through each chapter, we've broken down the essentials into bite-sized pieces, making it easier for you to digest and apply the information practically. This learning process marks an important stepping stone in your financial journey. Whether you're a working professional with limited time or a college student balancing studies and part-time work, your decision to pursue knowledge about investing is commendable.

One significant takeaway from your journey through this book is the importance of setting clear financial goals. It's crucial to define what you want to achieve with your investments. Setting specific, attainable objectives provides direction and purpose to your financial endeavors. Imagine the satisfaction of saving for a dream vacation or the joy of purchasing a new home. When you have a clear target in mind, it becomes easier to plan your investment strategy accordingly. Knowing what you want to achieve helps you stay focused, disciplined, and motivated.

While setting goals is vital, how you approach achieving them can make all the difference. Spreading your investments across different assets—also known as diversification—is a key principle that cannot be overstated. Think of your portfolio like a well-balanced meal. Just as various food groups contribute to a healthy diet, different types of investments can complement each other, providing balance and reducing risk. By diversifying, you are not putting all your eggs in one basket. This strategy helps protect your portfolio from volatility and unforeseen market changes, ensuring a smoother financial journey.

Additionally, diversification isn't just about mixing stocks; it's about blending various asset classes such as bonds, real estate, and mutual funds. Each asset type behaves differently under varying market conditions, and having a mix can help mitigate risks. As you continue investing, remember that diversification is not a one-time task but an ongoing process. It's important to regularly review and adjust your portfolio to align with changing market conditions and personal financial goals.

Staying informed and curious about the ever-evolving world of investing is another crucial aspect of successful investing. The stock market is dynamic, with new trends, opportunities, and risks emerging continually. Being a lifelong learner will serve you well in navigating this ever-changing landscape. Picture yourself as an enthusiastic student, always eager to absorb new information. Subscribe to financial news, attend webinars, join investment groups, and read books to expand your knowledge.

Commitment to continuous learning not only enhances your understanding but also keeps you prepared for making informed decisions. Knowledge equips you with the tools to analyze market trends, evaluate investment options, and adapt your strategies effectively. Never underestimate the power of staying current with financial news and educational resources. The more you learn, the better your chances of succeeding in the stock market.

It's also essential to stay grounded during this journey. Emotions can significantly impact investment decisions. Fear and greed are powerful emotions capable of clouding judgment and leading to irrational choices. Maintaining a balanced perspective and sticking to your planned strategy, especially during market fluctuations, is critical. Remember that ups and downs are inherent parts of investing. Keeping a level head during turbulent times will help you avoid impulsive decisions that could harm your long-term goals.

Take pride in the progress you've made so far, but also recognize that this is just the beginning. Investing is a lifelong endeavor. The principles you've learned here will serve as a strong foundation upon which you can build. Each experience, whether a success or a setback, will provide valuable lessons contributing to your growth as an investor.

Surround yourself with a support system—people who share your interests in investing. Engage in conversations about stocks, market trends, and financial goals. Such interactions can offer fresh perspectives, helping you learn and grow. Additionally, consider seeking advice from financial advisors when needed. Their expertise can guide you through complex scenarios and provide tailored strategies aligning with your unique goals.

Ultimately, the journey to financial prosperity is deeply personal. Everyone's path will differ based on their circumstances, risk tolerance, and aspirations. Be patient with yourself and trust the process. Celebrate your milestones, no matter how small they might seem. Every step forward is a victory moving you closer to your financial goals.

In conclusion, as you close this book, carry forward the wisdom gained and the confidence built. Your journey into the world of investing has only just begun. Stay focused, remain curious, and continue to learn. Set clear goals, diversify wisely, keep emotions in check, and surround yourself with supportive communities. With these guiding principles, you're well on your way to building a prosperous financial future. The stock market holds endless opportunities, and armed with your newfound knowledge, you are ready to seize them. Here's to your success and the exciting ventures that lie ahead!

References

Glossary | DataBank. databank.worldbank.org. (n.d.). https://dat abank.worldbank.org/metadataglossary/world-development-indicators/series/CM.MKT.LCAP.GD.ZS

Is Stock Market Concentration Rising? | *J.P. Morgan Research. www.jpmorgan.com.* (n.d.). http://chasechase.org/market-con centration.html

Understanding Financial Markets. William & Mary. (2023, July). https://online.mason.wm.edu/blog/understanding-financial-markets

CFP, M. (n.d.). *Stocks vs. Shares Defined: What's the Difference?. The Motley Fool.* http://thebalancesheet.org/index-1164.html

Comparing Bond Funds and Bond ETFs. Investopedia. (n.d.). http://file1040nr.org/pros-cons-bond-funds-vs-bond-etfs. html

Falk, J. (2022, June). *Why is the stock market falling? A Mercer finance expert explains and offers advice. The Den.* https://den. mercer.edu/why-is-the-stock-market-falling-a-mercer-fin ance-expert-explains-and-offers-advice/

Market Indices. www.sec.gov. (n.d.). https://www.sec.gov/answ
ers/indices.htm

*Stock Market Index : Features, Examples, Need & Major Stock
Indices. GeeksforGeeks.* (2024, March). https://www.geeksf
orgeeks.org/stock-market-index-features-examples-need-
major-stock-indices/

The Office of Financial Readiness. finred.usalearning.gov. (n.d.).
https://finred.usalearning.gov/Saving/StocksBondsMutualFu
nds

*What Are Equities or Equity Investments? - SmartAsset | SmartAsset.
www.eveningoptimistclubofsumter.org.* (n.d.). http://www.eveni
ngoptimistclubofsumter.org/what-are-equities.html

*6 Best Investment Accounts for Handling Uninvested Cash. Investo-
pedia.* (n.d.). http://www.shava.org/best-investment-account
s-uninvested-cash-7486554.html

*Are Two Brokerages Preferable to One? - Bogleheads.org.
www.bogleheads.org.* (n.d.). https://www.bogleheads.org/
forum/viewtopic.php?t=411425

Best Stock Screeners for May 2024. Investopedia. (n.d.). http://ww
w.file1040nr.org/best-stock-screeners-5120586.html

*Financial Goal-Setting: The Key to Building Wealth (Rutgers NJAES).
njaes.rutgers.edu.* (n.d.). https://njaes.rutgers.edu/sshw/messa

ge/message.php?p=Finance&m=124

Investment Goals | FINRA.org. www.finra.org. (n.d.). https://www.finra.org/investors/investing/investing-basics/investment-goals

What Are Stock Fundamentals?. Investopedia. (n.d.). http://www.file1040nr.org/022603.html

Best Stock Screeners for May 2024. Investopedia. (n.d.). http://www.file1040nr.org/best-stock-screeners-5120586.html

*Customizing Stock Scanners and Screeners for Personal Use. * (2024, May). https://www.asmarterchoice.org/customizing-stock-scanners-and-screeners-for-personal-use/

Methods of Stock Market Prediction | Lisa Hladik: Senior Capstone Project. muse.union.edu. (n.d.). https://muse.union.edu/2019capstone-hladikl/methods-of-stock-market-prediction-2/

Santa Clara University. (2023, September). *Introduction to Financial Analysis. SCU.* https://onlinedegrees.scu.edu/media/blog/introduction-to-financial-analysis

What Is Intrinsic Value of Stock and How to Calculate It?. LiteFinance. (n.d.). https://www.litefinance.org/blog/for-beginners/what-is-fundamental-analysis/intrinsic-value/

Aly, S., Attia, E., Awad, E., ElRawas, A. (2023, June). *Portfolio diversification benefits before and during the times of COVID-19: evidence from USA. Future Business Journal.* None

Asset Allocation with Real-World Constraints. www.cfainstitute.org. (n.d.). https://www.cfainstitute.org/en/membership/professi onal-development/refresher-readings/asset-allocation-real-world-constraints

Diversification of Investment : Meaning, How it Works & Importance. GeeksforGeeks. (2024, February). https://www.geeksfo rgeeks.org/diversification-of-investment-meaning-how-it-works-importance/

FINRA. (n.d.). *Asset Allocation and Diversification | FINRA.org. www.finra.org.* https://www.finra.org/investors/investing/inv esting-basics/asset-allocation-diversification

SEC.gov | Beginners' Guide to Asset Allocation, Diversification, and Rebalancing. www.sec.gov. (2009, August). https://www.sec.go v/about/reports-publications/investor-publications/investor -pubs-asset-allocation

Caplinger, D. (n.d.). *The Basics of Value Investing Strategy. The Motley Fool.* http://thebalancesheet.org/index-1160.html

How to Spot an Undervalued Stock – SmartAsset | SmartAsset. abroker.org. (n.d.). http://abroker.org/undervalued-stock.ht ml

Investment Strategies to Learn Before Trading. Investopedia. (n.d.). http://www.file1040nr.org/index-5.html

Khan Academy. (n.d.). *Short, medium, and long term goals (article). Khan Academy.* https://www.khanacademy.org/colle

ge-careers-more/financial-literacy/xa6995ea67a8e9fdd:fin
ancial-goals/xa6995ea67a8e9fdd:short-medium-and-long-
term-goals/a/short-medium-and-long-term-goals

*Short-Term vs. Long-Term Certificates | Benchmark FCU. *
(2024, February). https://www.benchmarkfcu.org/short-term
-vs-long-term-certificates/

U.S. SECURITIES and EXCHANGE COMMISSION. (2015). *Ten
Things to Consider Before You Make Investing Decisions. Sec.gov.*
https://www.sec.gov/investor/pubs/tenthingstoconsider.htm

retirebyforty. (2013, January). *Building A Dividend Portfolio For
Passive Income. Retire by 40.* https://retireby40.org/dividend-
portfolio-passive-income/

6 Steps to Consider During Volatile Markets. Schwab Brokerage.
(n.d.). http://madmacraffle.org/6-steps-to-consider-during-
volatile-markets.html

*How to Hedge Against an Event-Driven Market Correction. Schwab
Brokerage.* (n.d.). http://madmacraffle.org/how-to-hedge-yo
ur-portfolio.html

*Six Tips to Manage Market Volatility for Investments › 1st United
Credit Union. www.1stunitedcu.org.* (n.d.). https://www.1stunite
dcu.org/more-for-you/financial-wellness/six-tips-to-mana
ge-market-volatility-for-investments

10 Best AI Tools for Stock Market Analysis [2024]. GeeksforGeeks.
(2024, January). https://www.geeksforgeeks.org/ai-tools-for-

stock-market-analysis/

Best Online Stocks Courses and Programs. edX. (n.d.). https://ww
w.edx.org/learn/stocks

*How I Generate Investment Ideas. CFA Institute Enterprising
Investor.* (2019, April). https://blogs.cfainstitute.org/investor/
2019/04/08/how-i-generate-investment-ideas/

Investment Strategies to Learn Before Trading. Investopedia. (n.d.).
http://www.file1040nr.org/index-5.html

Klusek, L. (2023). *Research Guides: Porter's Five Forces Analysis:
Threat of Substitution. guides.newman.baruch.cuny.edu.* https://g
uides.newman.baruch.cuny.edu/c.php?g=188285&p=1244359

Research Writing Process (Book). Bismarckschools.org. (2019).
https://learnbps.bismarckschools.org/mod/book/tool/print/
index.php?id=89418

Team, P. (2023, October). *Learning the Ropes: Educational
Resources in Investment Communities - Publish What You Pay.
* https://www.publishwhatyoupay.org/learning-the-ropes-e
ducational-resources-in-investment-communities/